FISCAL SPONSORSHIP

6 Ways To Do It Right

SECOND EDITION

BY GREGORY L. COLVIN

SILK, ADLER & COLVIN

FIRST EDITION JOINTLY FUNDED BY
THE SAN FRANCISCO FOUNDATION
THE WALLACE ALEXANDER GERBODE FOUNDATION

WITH THE PARTICIPATION OF
CALIFORNIA LAWYERS FOR THE ARTS • FILM ARTS FOUNDATION
INTERSECTION FOR THE ARTS • SAN FRANCISCO STUDY CENTER

STUDY CENTER PRESS

Editor: Geoffrey Link
Designer: Lenny Limjoco
San Francisco Study Center

Study Center Press
1095 Market St., Suite 602
San Francisco, CA 94103
Fax: (415) 626-7276
1-888-281-3757
info@studycenter.org

Library of Congress Control Number: 2005927450
ISBN 1-888956-07-0 (Paper)
ISBN 1-888956-08-9 (Cloth)
Second Edition, Revised and Enlarged

CONTENTS

PREFACE

Welcome to the second edition of *Fiscal Sponsorship: 6 Ways To Do It Right*.

The first edition was published in 1993 after a period of controversy in the nonprofit world about an arrangement often called "fiscal agency." This term actually referred to several different constructs, but the common theme was that some enterprising person or group wished to conduct a charitable program and fund it with tax-deductible contributions, but without incorporating or obtaining Internal Revenue Service recognition of the project's Internal Revenue Code Section 501(c)(3) tax exemption. An existing 501(c)(3) "fiscal agent" would be recruited to receive grants and donations to support the project, then disburse the funds in the form of payments to employees, vendors, contractors or grantees.

These arrangements, if not handled carefully, were vulnerable to the criticism that the fiscal agents were mere conduits for the transmission of deductible donations to entities not qualified to receive them.

Since publication of the book, the term "fiscal sponsorship" has become accepted as a more appropriate label for arrangements done correctly. In the last decade, the phenomenon of fiscal sponsorship has become common, widespread, and quite reputable. It has become a popular ancillary activity for public charities involved in human service, environmental, artistic, and many other community endeavors. Nonprofit 501(c)(3) institutions solely devoted to fiscal sponsorship have sprung up across the country, ranging from documentary film sponsors to public health research groups to separate sponsorship corporations spun off by community foundations.

Fortunately, no significant changes in the aspects of tax-exempt or nonprofit law that bear upon fiscal sponsorship have occurred since this book was first published in 1993, so readers can continue to rely on the first edition as a valid expression of the legal principles underlying fiscal sponsorship.

Therefore, the original main text is reprinted in this 2005 edition virtually unchanged, except for updates to legal citations, clarifying phraseology and correction of typos.

However, this edition contains a new, extended Postscript entitled "Lessons Learned, Concepts Clarified, Recent Developments" beginning on page 62. It outlines a number of significant developments, improvements in theory and practice, and advanced techniques of fiscal sponsorship that have come to light in the meantime.

Also, the items in the Appendix are virtually unchanged from the 1993 book, so that users of the original book can be assured that the relationships they may have properly created in the past are still valid.

Beyond that, we intend to take full advantage of the electronic age to help readers, advisors and practitioners of fiscal sponsorship gain access to the latest thinking in the field. With the release of this edition, the San Francisco Study Center is launching and will host a Website at www.fiscalsponsorship.com. As interesting new developments occur in fiscal sponsorship, they will be posted at this site so that the public will not need to wait for the next edition to learn about them. The site will also link to the Study Center's developing national directory of fiscal sponsors and other resources.

Separately, the Silk, Adler & Colvin Website, www.silklaw.com, will present a variety of fiscal sponsorship agreements and other documents as exemplars for the use of lawyers and accountants who advise fiscal sponsors, funding sources and sponsored projects.

We hope that this second edition, along with the new Web-based functions, will lead to more intense, systematic and broad-scale efforts to "build out" the potential of fiscal sponsorship as a platform for the incubation, consolidation, support — and sometimes instant creation — of new charitable enterprises in the 21st century.

Greg Colvin
Silk, Adler & Colvin
August 2005

ACKNOWLEDGEMENTS*

The first expressions of interest in a book of this kind arose in meetings among representatives of four leading San Francisco fiscal sponsors in the arts and human services: Frances Phillips of Intersection for the Arts, Geoff Link of San Francisco Study Center, Julie Mackaman of Film Arts Foundation, and Alma Robinson of California Lawyers for the Arts. With able assistance from John Kreidler of The San Francisco Foundation and Tom Layton of The Wallace Alexander Gerbode Foundation, these four groups began a series of meetings in 1991 to collect and share information on sponsorship practices to clarify their legal underpinnings and improve their effectiveness. Throughout the writing of this book, they have been an invaluable source of concrete experience and helpful critiques, keeping the focus on enabling a variety of charitable projects to succeed within the parameters of the law.

When the first draft was completed, it was circulated to a number of knowledgeable and nationally prominent nonprofit experts for review. Those who responded with thoughtful suggestions, encouragement and criticism included John Edie, Marcus Owens, Mort Levy, Drummond Pike, Kirke Wilson, Bill Lehrfeld, Deirdre Dessingue, Bob Smucker and Michael O'Neill.

Within our law firm, my associates Rosemary Fei and Rob Wexler contributed research and rewriting support, and my partners Tom Silk and Betsy Adler were masterful editors. The man who founded the firm, Tom Silk, is truly the inspiration for this book, because it was he who pioneered the approach of providing clients with alternative legal models for sponsors and projects to work together, and successfully defended them in negotiations with the Internal Revenue Service.

---

*Many of the people important in the making of the first edition remain close to the project today. This section opens with an abbreviated acknowledgement from 1993, and concludes with an update of the major players' continuing roles.

Looking back at the Acknowledgements from 1993, noticing what has changed and what has remained the same, is itself an historical exercise that shows the impressive evolution of fiscal sponsorship.

In the San Francisco Bay Area, Intersection for the Arts, the San Francisco Study Center, Film Arts Foundation and California Lawyers for the Arts have all matured and intensified their fiscal sponsorship services. The San Francisco Foundation and the Gerbode Foundation continue to be strong patrons of fiscally sponsored projects.

In particular, The San Francisco Foundation has broken new ground as the first community foundation to spin off its sponsored projects into a separate nonprofit corporation, The San Francisco Foundation Community Initiative Funds (CIF), in 1996. CIF's assets, annual revenues and expenses are now in the $10 million range, and it sponsors more than 50 projects, mainly Model A direct projects with some Model B independent contracts and Model C regrant relationships. Now renamed CIF of The San Francisco Foundation, this successful program intends to package its unique mode of service and offer a CIF manual to community foundations in other cities. I have been proud to serve as a director and officer of CIF since its inception, and have admired the dedicated leadership that David Barlow, Jan Masaoka, John Kreidler and Leslie Hume provide CIF year after year. CIF has become an invaluable laboratory for creatively advancing the theory and practice of fiscal sponsorship; many of the "lessons learned" in the Postscript come directly from the CIF experiment.

From the original *Fiscal Sponsorship* team, Geoff Link has been a loyal and enthusiastic editor, publisher and marketer of this book, patiently waiting for the updated manuscript, while keeping the book in print for those who needed it and continued to buy at least one copy a day during the 12 years between editions.

Frances Phillips, still a strong supporter of fiscal sponsorship, now directs the Creative Work Fund. Julie Mackaman is an arts consultant on the East Coast.

Many of the nationally prominent nonprofit experts who reviewed the initial book have continued to care about and promote better fiscal sponsorship.

John Edie gave us the unforgettable image of the fiscal agent who provides nothing more than "a warm room with a copy of IRS Publication 78 on the shelf."

Marcus Owens, having left his post as chief of Exempt Organizations at the IRS for the law firm of Caplin & Drysdale, remains a good friend.

Drummond Pike of Tides Foundation guided the spin-off of Tides Center, now a separate corporation devoted to fiscal sponsorship nationwide and the recipient of a substantial grant from the W.K. Kellogg Foundation to improve its sponsorship facilities and identify best practices in the field.

Bill Lehrfeld has, sadly, passed away, but his legacy of cutting-edge litigation includes *Fund for Anonymous Gifts v. U.S.*, a case that has helped define donor-advised funds and, indirectly, fiscal sponsorship.

To this list must be added Victoria Bjorklund and Celia Roady, colleagues from the American Bar Association, Tax Section, Exempt Organizations Committee, who have always been on the lookout for opportunities to make fiscal sponsorship better known and understood.

Thanks also to the Foundation Center Library and the Council on Foundations, who saw the value of the original edition and kept promoting it faithfully to their book buyers.

Within our law firm, since 1993, Rosemary Fei, Rob Wexler, Erik Dryburgh and Ingrid Mittermaier have joined Tom Silk, Betsy Adler and me as owners, allowing us to specialize in fiscal sponsorship as well as many other subareas of nonprofit law. Over the years, our hard-working associates Greg Siegler, Alice Anderson and Stephanie Petit, along with the financial wizard Terry Miller, supported, deepened and challenged our thinking. And you couldn't wish for a better secretary than Kay Bush, or a better research librarian than Angela Moore-Evans.

Finally, my love and appreciation to my wife, Donna, my sons, Jared and Chris, and our daughter, Juliet, who is now 6 years old and for whom I must end this sentence to get home before she goes to bed.

Greg Colvin
August 2005

PARTICIPATING ORGANIZATIONS

The San Francisco Foundation
225 Bush Street, Suite 500
San Francisco, CA 94104
www.sff.org

Wallace A. Gerbode Foundation
111 Pine Street, Suite 1515
San Francisco, CA 94111
www.fdncenter.org/grantmaker/gerbode

California Lawyers for the Arts
Fort Mason Center
Building C, Room 255
San Francisco, CA 94123
www.calawyersforthearts.org

Intersection for the Arts
446 Valencia Street
San Francisco, CA 94103
www.theintersection.org

San Francisco Study Center
1095 Market Street, Suite 602
San Francisco, CA 94103
www.studycenter.org

Film Arts Foundation
145 Ninth Street, Suite 101
San Francisco, CA 94103
www.filmarts.org

Address comments to:

Gregory L. Colvin
Silk, Adler & Colvin
235 Montgomery Street, Suite 1220
San Francisco, CA 94104

(415) 421-7555   Fax: (415) 421-0712
Or visit Websites:
www.fiscalsponsorship.com
www.silklaw.com

FOREWORD TO THE FIRST EDITION

One objective of the nonprofit sector is to produce goods and services in a manner that is both efficient and publicly accountable. If a program is to be operated over a long time span, it often is desirable to establish an independent nonprofit organization to provide an institutional framework to accommodate both program and administrative activities. For a temporary project or one for which a long-term need is not yet assured, it may be inappropriate, even wasteful, to construct a new nonprofit organization, even though the intended product or service fits the legal definition of "nonprofit." In such cases, a fiscal sponsorship arrangement with an existing nonprofit organization may be established to attain an effective base for operations.

For decades, fiscal sponsorship arrangements have been used to carry out, legally and efficiently, programs possessing far-reaching public significance:

• Many projects carried out by researchers, filmmakers, video artists, small performing ensembles, writers and scientists are sponsored by nonprofit organizations. Major universities often maintain "sponsored projects" offices to support the work of their faculty and staff. In the world of the arts, the New York Foundation for the Arts, the Film Arts Foundation, Intersection for the Arts and many other longstanding organizations have developed highly refined programs of fiscal sponsorship that annually support the work of hundreds of individuals and small groups.

• Community foundations throughout the nation serve as fiscal sponsors for a multitude of projects. The San Francisco Foundation manages the financial and administrative affairs of 39 separate projects involving independent living for senior citizens, a capital campaign for a new Main Library, and a host of other accounts. At the request of the National Endowment for the Arts, The San Francisco Foundation served as the collection point for $2.2 million in contributions from individuals, foundations, corporations and government agencies for the relief of artists and arts organizations affected by the devastating earthquake that rocked the San Francisco Bay Area in October 1989.

One rationale that underlies most fiscal sponsorship arrangements is strictly legalistic: few funding organizations and individual contributors will donate funds to worthy public projects that lack tax-exempt status. Yet many organizations that operate regular programs of fiscal sponsorship provide their sponsored projects with far more than just legal status. Oftentimes, the sponsor provides accounting, payroll, employee benefits, office space, equipment, publicity and fund-raising assistance free or at cost. Providing these services spares projects the necessity of developing their own administrative expertise and resources, thereby freeing them to focus more on programming and financial efficiency than otherwise would be possible.

Despite its long history, extensive utilization, and potential for efficiency and productivity, a stigma is often attached to the very concept of fiscal sponsorship. Some view it as a tax dodge: a shady sleight-of-hand to slip funds to activities that do not truly qualify as charitable. Indeed, abuses have occurred, though probably in most cases the problem is not malfeasance, but rather ignorance of the rights and responsibilities of the three participating parties: the donor, the sponsor and the project. Moreover, many of the variant approaches to fiscal sponsorship are unknown even to veterans of the non-profit sector. With proper understanding, these alternate approaches could be employed in appropriate projects to achieve even better results.

With these problems and opportunities in mind, Tom Layton, director of The Wallace Alexander Gerbode Foundation, and I convened a group of directors of organizations with well-established fiscal sponsorship programs to exchange information. This led to a conversation between Tom and Greg Colvin, a partner in the San Francisco law firm of Silk, Adler & Colvin, about the potential for a publication on fiscal sponsorship that would have wide appeal. We commissioned Greg's firm to write a booklet, which grew into this book. Book production was managed by the San Francisco Study Center, itself a highly talented fiscal sponsor of research and publication projects involving public issues.

John Kreidler, Senior Program Executive
The San Francisco Foundation, April 1993

INTRODUCTION

NOT FISCAL AGENCY

This book is concerned with how to maximize the philanthropic community's ability to support important activities, from arts to international aid, from environmental activism to individual health needs, and a host of other human services.

In the last 10 years, public charities, community foundations and private foundations have become increasingly worried about the future of a funding practice widely (and unfortunately) known as "fiscal agency."

That practice has been criticized in articles[1], so much so that some organizations have considered abandoning the practice. Most have continued it, however, for the compelling reason that the charitable sector would be crippled without a way to harness the creativity and respond to the needs of a vast array of groups and individuals that lack the tax-exempt status required to receive grants from many private foundations, government agencies and other funders.

> ### Get good advice
>
> This publication is intended to orient a variety of charities to the possibilities for legal, effective fiscal sponsorship programs. It is not intended to provide legal advice directly to any specific organization. You will need professional legal and accounting advice to help you establish, review or modify a fiscal sponsorship program.

The purpose of this book is to take a positive approach to the problem. It describes, in general terms, six different models (plus a seventh, experimental model) by which a public charity, tax-exempt under Section 501(c)(3) of the Internal Revenue Code (IRC), can conduct a program of support to individuals and to nonexempt organizations that is legal and proper.

First, a change in terminology is needed to reflect the proper relation-

---

[1] See, for example, "Use of Fiscal Agents: A Trap for the Unwary," by John A. Edie, Council on Foundations (1989).

---

ships. The arrangement should not be called "fiscal agency," because the charity is not, and should not be, the legal agent of the nonexempt project. Under the law of agency, an agent acts on behalf of another (the principal) who has the right to direct and control the agent's activities. Calling a charity a "fiscal agent" implies that the project controls the charity. To comply with tax-exempt law, the relationship must be the reverse; the charity must be in the controlling position, and the nonexempt project must act so as to further the charity's exempt purposes.

Fiscal sponsorship is the more accurate term. It implies, correctly, that the charity has made a choice to support the nonexempt project financially.

Fiscal sponsorship arrangements typically arise when a person or group (we will call this **a project**) wants to get support from a private foundation, a government agency, or tax-deductible donations from individual or corporate donors. By law or preference, the funding source will make payments only to organizations with 501(c)(3) tax status. So the project looks for a 501(c)(3) **sponsor** to receive the funds and pass them on to the project.

However, the IRS has a strict policy against "conduit" arrangements. When A makes a donation to B, earmarked for C (the project), it is in reality a donation from A to C. But if C is not exempt under Section 501(c)(3), the gift is not a tax-deductible contribution. To be deductible, the IRS requires that B (the sponsor) have "complete discretion and control" over the funds, and holds the sponsor legally responsible to see that its payments to the project further the sponsor's tax-exempt purposes.[2]

> ## How charities grow
>
> This work is, ultimately, about the vigor of the charitable sector in the United States. It catches the charitable enterprise at a stage in which the growth of its public benefit activities has outpaced the development of the usual accompanying legal structure. As we hope this book demonstrates, existing charitable organizations, equipped with a knowledge of available legal options, can play a vital role in nurturing the young charitable enterprise — an essential component of a dynamic and flourishing charitable sector.
>
> — *Tom Silk,* partner
> Silk, Adler & Colvin

---

[2] *S.E. Thomason v. Commissioner*, 2 T.C. 441 (1943); Rev. Rul. 54-580, 1954-2 C.B. 97; Rev. Rul. 63-252, 1963-2 C.B. 101; Rev. Rul. 66-79, 1966-1 C.B. 48; *National Foundation v. U.S.*, 13 Cl. Ct. 486, 87-2 USTC ¶9602 (1987); IRS Private Letter Ruling 9247030.

As the models demonstrate, fiscal sponsorship advantages are not limited to situations where the project lacks, or never will have, 501(c)(3) status. Fiscal sponsorship is often temporary, used for that period before a new organization obtains its own tax exemption. Other variations occur when a small 501(c)(3) group needs a larger 501(c)(3) organization to manage its financial affairs or seeks IRS classification as a public charity based on its relationship with the sponsor.

These models are not etched in stone. Consider them simply devices for understanding the possibilities. Each model is really a paradigm with certain unique characteristics. In practice, they may be used in combinations, blended, subdivided, and they may serve as springboards for developing new models.

To provide concrete examples of how a proper fiscal sponsorship program can be constructed, we start with three hypothetical situations.

HYPOTHETICAL SITUATIONS

#1: THE ARTISTS

Amparo Sanchez is a young dancer and choreographer who has been adapting traditional Native American and Latin American dance forms. She wants to found a dance troupe. Keith Carson is a budding filmmaker who wants to produce a documentary film featuring Sanchez's work, to be shown on public television and used in classrooms. Their intent is to advance dance and film as art forms, and to educate the general public.

The City Arts Consortium, a Section 501(c)(3) public charity, was formed to promote artistic and cultural endeavors. Amparo and Keith have asked the consortium for fiscal sponsorship, so that each of them can obtain funding from government grants, private foundations, and from wealthy individuals for their projects.

Amparo wants to raise $25,000 annually to subsidize her dance troupe, which will also raise money by charging admission for public performances, and eventually she wants her troupe to be an independent, nonprofit, self-sustaining arts organization.

Keith is seeking $100,000, half for the personal services of himself, Amparo, dancers, musicians and various technicians, and half for costumes, studio space, camera rental and other expenses. When the film is done, Keith wants to own it and control its distribution.

The consortium would like to establish a fiscal sponsorship program to support projects like Amparo's and Keith's, with a 10% sponsorship charge and a provision for repayment from the film's revenues if it ever turns a profit.

#2: THE HUMAN SERVICES PROJECT

As the leading charitable institution in its small community, the Angel Island Community Church has been asked to assist a number of self-help and mutual-aid projects created by people on the island. Several years ago, a group of people with AIDS and members of the congregation set up a program for terminally ill people, Community Church Hospice.

The church has encouraged the development of the hospice; however, from the outset, the church made clear it could not afford to fund the hospice. So, with outside contributions, donations from patients, and earmarked bequests to the church, the hospice project became self-funding.

Initially, the ill were cared for in spare rooms in the homes of the church members. Before long the need far outstripped the available space. The hospice, in the name of the church, received a care contract from the village government of Angel Island, and rented a large house that it renovated to fit beds for 12.

With the hospice have come problems for the church. The part-time bookkeeper has complained that the hospice is now so large that she doesn't have time to keep track of its financial transactions, and she is not sure she knows enough to do it correctly anyhow. The minister and the church's governing body are concerned about continuing to operate the hospice within the church, considering the hospice's growth and increasing number of legal questions that are beyond their expertise. For instance, some hospice patients' parents have telephoned from back East to ask whether they can make a charitable contribution to the church to help pay the high cost of medicine for their son or daughter.

#3: THE ENVIRONMENTAL GROUP

Holly and Sweet William, famous for their herbal tea company, have assembled a group of people who call themselves the Friends of the Brazilian Rain Forest (FBRF). The group knows that it would not qualify for 501(c)(3) tax-exemption because it intends to lobby extensively in the United States, Brazil and other countries for legislation preserving threatened rain forest areas, and programs of aid to the indigenous peoples of the rain forest. Instead, it will apply for 501(c)(4) tax status as a social welfare organization, to which contributors may not make tax-deductible donations.

Holly wants to make a large donation to enable FBRF to preserve a certain 68-square-mile area in Brazil from destruction by supporting litigation, lobbying and the local native community organization. It happens that Holly and Sweet William's company receives most of its supply of certain herbs from this region.

Holly wants her donation to be tax-deductible, so FBRF has asked the Cordillera Club Foundation, a U.S. 501(c)(3) public charity, to be its fiscal sponsor. The foundation is considering accepting the donation, paying part of it over to the FBRF and part directly to the local Brazilian community organization.

Also, a Mormon missionary who lives there and serves the native people is an important contact person for FBRF. She needs more money to stay another two years in Brazil, and her parents want to know how they can make tax-deductible payments for her living expenses to enable her to do so.

THE MODELS

SUMMARY

All of the models summarized in the accompanying chart represent legal ways in which a project can derive some benefit from a relationship with a sponsor.

The chart places the model with the least financial independence for the project at the top (Model A, Direct Project) and the model with the most financial independence for the project at the bottom (Model F, Technical Assistance). The seventh model (X) has had limited use so far, and its broader application is uncertain.

In Models A (Direct Project) and B (Independent Contractor Project) the project is an integral part of the sponsor's program activities. They differ on the issue of whether the people conducting the project may be legally classified as independent contractors or as employees.

Model C (Preapproved Grant) is a grantor-grantee relationship between the sponsor and the project. This includes the one-time arrangement enabling a project to obtain the proceeds of a grant from a private foundation via a sponsor, as well as the ongoing arrangement where a sponsor receives and transfers funds to a project as funds are raised.

Model D (Group Exemption) and Model E (Supporting Organization) are advanced models that result in the project having its own 501(c)(3) tax status, able to receive deductible donations directly from donors, but still with a tax benefit derived from the sponsor. The main tax difference between them is this: With the Group Exemption, the project gets 501(c)(3) status by coming under the sponsor's umbrella, but the project must meet a public support test. Conversely, the Supporting Organization applies for its own 501(c)(3) status, but does not need to show public support since its public charity status is derived from its relationship to the sponsor.

The Model F (Technical Assistance) project has its own 501(c)(3) status and all funds are handled in the name of the project, but financial management assistance is provided by the sponsor whose employees are skilled in payroll, bookkeeping, tax returns and other administrative details.

Model X (Payments "For the Use of" Sponsor) is a concept derived from a 1990 U.S. Supreme Court decision involving Mormon missionaries. The ruling appears to allow donors to make deductible contributions not directly to a charity sponsor, but to a separate account set up by the project in trust for the sponsor.

After describing each model, we will apply the models to the three hypothetical examples. The choice of model does not depend on whether the project involves art, health or the environment, but upon making a good match between a specific administrative system and the sponsor's and the project's long-term goals.

FISCAL SPONSORSHIP MODELS	BASIC CHARACTERISTICS	IS PROJECT LEGAL ENTITY?	BASIC RELATIONSHIP	CHARITABLE DONATIONS BELONG TO
A. **DIRECT PROJECT**	Project belongs to sponsor and is implemented by its employees and volunteers.	No	Employer-Employee	Sponsor
B. **INDEPENDENT CONTRACTOR PROJECT**	Project belongs to sponsor but is conducted by separate entity under contract.	Yes	Project contract	Sponsor
C. **PREAPPROVED GRANT RELATIONSHIP**	Project applies to sponsor for one or a series of grants, sponsor funds project only to extent that money is received from donors.	Yes	Grantor-Grantee	Sponsor
D. **GROUP EXEMPTION**	Sponsor obtains federal group tax exemption, confers 501(c)(3) status on subordinate projects.	Yes	Subordinate-Affiliate	Project
E. **SUPPORTING ORGANIZATION**	Project gets its own 501(c)(3) exemption, but public charity status is based on support of sponsor's purposes.	Yes	Degree of connection varies	Project
F. **TECHNICAL ASSISTANCE**	· Project has its own 501(c)(3) exemption but needs help with bookkeeping, tax returns, payroll, management, etc.	Yes	Management contract	Project
X. **PAYMENTS "FOR THE USE OF" SPONSOR**	Project approved by sponsor, trust account is set up for project separate from sponsor's assets, donors pay directly to trust account.	May or may not be	Sponsor must control project	Project in trust for sponsor

SPONSOR'S LIABILITY TO 3RD PARTIES	OWNERSHIP OF RESULTS	PAYMENTS SHOWN ON IRS RETURNS FILED BY		COMMENTS
		SPONSOR	PROJECT	
Total liability for acts of employees.	Sponsor	990, payroll tax returns	Individual 1040s	Legally, project is no different than any other activity carried on by sponsor directly.
Varies, may be partial or total.	Should be conveyed to sponsor	990, 1099 if person	Depends on contractor's legal status	Appropriate where project is integral to sponsor's work, may be legally done by independent contractor.
Selection and payment of grantee, plus terms set by funding source.	Project usually	990	Depends on grantee's legal status	Used by non-501(c)(3) project, in order to raise tax-deductible support from donors, private foundations or government grants.
Only as provided in affiliation agreement.	Project	Annual listing of orgs., no financial information.	990, separate or group return	Project gets 501(c)(3) status without separate application to IRS; under sponsor's supervision/control.
None.	Project	None	990	Project must apply to IRS for 501(c)(3) status, but can be a public charity even with only one donor.
Only as provided in contract.	Project	990 if fee charged	990 if fee paid	Sponsor provides financial management to project, but all funds are raised and spent in the name of project.
Varies, may be partial or total.	Project in trust for sponsor	None	Depends on trust's legal status	New, untested model based on U.S. Supreme Court decision on acceptable methods for Mormon parents to aid missionary children.

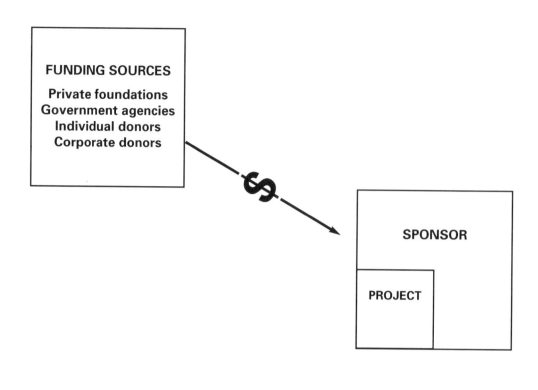

FUNDING SOURCES

Private foundations
Government agencies
Individual donors
Corporate donors

SPONSOR

PROJECT

MODEL A — DIRECT PROJECT

In Model A, the sponsor takes the project in-house. The project has no separate legal existence. The originators of the project may have approached the sponsor with a program idea that had not been part of the sponsor's activities in the past, but once the sponsor adopts it as a staff project, it belongs completely to the sponsor. These fiscal sponsors see themselves often as "incubators" for new charities, or "umbrella" organizations permitting several related projects to exist under one tax-exempt corporation.

Model A is probably the most common form of institutionalized fiscal sponsorship. Model A provides the most control over the project, and is the least exposed to IRS challenge, so it is the best training ground for start-up projects. Some legal problems do occur, however, when the project decides to go off on its own, if the sponsor and project do not have a clear understanding at the outset of what the terms of eventual separation will be.[3] As we shall see, Model A is most suitable for Amparo's dance troupe, allowing her to focus on the artistic and program development of her group, while learning from the sponsor how to administer a charitable enterprise.

Relationship

The people conducting the project become employees or volunteers of the sponsor for the duration of the project. Project expenses are paid directly by the sponsor to vendors and suppliers. This is so even if a separate bank account is set up for the project. The bank account belongs to the sponsor, even if project staff are signatories on the account. As employer of the project personnel, the sponsor's board of directors is ultimately responsible for over-seeing their activities. Payroll tax withholding, workers' compensation insurance, unemployment benefits, and the sponsor's personnel policies also apply to the project staff as well as to the sponsor's regular staff.

Handling of Charitable Donations

The project personnel may take the lead in writing grant requests and soliciting donations. In this fund-raising role, even before they become employees, they are making representations on behalf of the sponsor. They may be regarded as agents of the sponsor with the result that commitments made by them may be binding on the sponsor. The sponsor, therefore, should review all fund-raising materials prepared by the project in the name of the sponsor before they are used. All checks should be made payable to the spon-sor. All funds raised are the property of the sponsor. Depending on the com-mitments made to grantors and donors, the sponsor may be required to treat money designated for the project as a restricted fund on its financial records and on its Form 990 tax return. If so, charitable trust law and contract law hold that the funds may not be diverted to another purpose.

---

[3] This issue is addressed in the subsequent section, "Leaving the Model A Nest."

Administrative Charge

The sponsor may decide that a certain percentage of the funds raised shall not be passed on to the project, but shall be kept for the sponsor's general administration and overhead, so long as this does not contravene any agreements made with grantors or donors.[4]

Liabilities

Because the project is an integral part of the sponsor, its activities create the same liabilities for the sponsor as would any other program. The sponsor is liable for the actions and omissions of project employees, within the scope of their employment. If the project has unpaid bills, borrows money, injures someone, damages property, infringes someone's copyright, or undertakes the obligation to supply goods or services to others — all these are the sponsor's liabilities.

Ownership

If the project buys equipment, furniture, buildings, land, works of art, or other tangible assets, they belong to the sponsor. Likewise, if the project acquires or its work results in the creation of intangible assets, such as copyrights, options, or trademarks, those also are property of the sponsor.

Tax Reporting

All of the financial transactions involving the project go through the sponsor's accounting systems and appear on the sponsor's IRS Form 990 tax return. Payroll tax returns must also be filed for employee compensation. As for the employed project personnel, they simply receive salary or wages, which they report on their own IRS Form 1040 tax returns.

---

[4] Administrative charges customarily range from 5% to 15%.

APPLYING MODEL A TO THE HYPOTHETICALS

#1 — The Artists

The City Arts Consortium could be the perfect "incubator" for Amparo's dance troupe during its early years. Amparo can raise charitable funds as "a project of" the Arts Consortium. The consortium could use 10% of the money raised for its general purposes, and delegate control of 90% of the funds to Amparo, subject to the ultimate control of the consortium's board of directors. Amparo and her dance troupe will be employees and volunteers of the consortium, and she will need to abide by the financial procedures established by the sponsor to administer her expenditures. While the project is within the consortium, all admission fees from public performances are the property of the consortium as well.

If the Arts Consortium makes the film a direct project, Amparo, Keith and the other people needed to make the film will become its employees. If the film goes over budget and there are unpaid bills, or copyright infringements occur, the sponsor is liable. The film, as a "work made for hire," is the property of the sponsor, which has the right to control its distribution. The contributions of others to the film, such as the musical score, are the property of the sponsor unless, for instance, the composer is an independent contractor who insists on retaining copyright. All revenues from the film belong to the sponsor. While Model A will work to provide fiscal sponsorship for the film, it will not meet Keith's goal of owning the film himself, although the consortium may allow him considerable latitude to manage the film's distribution.

#2 — The Human Services Project

In this example, the hospice was established by the church as a direct project. The donations and bequests received by the church for the hospice project should be accounted for as restricted funds. The contract for patient care with the village of Angel Island is the church's obligation to perform, and the lease on the hospice facility belongs to the church.

This hypothetical presents the situation of a Model A direct project that has outgrown its sponsor's ability to manage it. The most obvious cure for the problem is to create a separate nonprofit corporation for the hospice project, which would obtain its own 501(c)(3) status, and to transfer the assets and liabilities (with the consent of third parties such as the village government) from the church to the new corporation following the steps suggested in the next section on "leaving the nest." However, as will be explained later, this is not the only answer. Several of the other models may apply so that a complete separation may not be needed.

#3 — The Environmental Group

In this situation, the activities that the Friends of the Brazilian Rain Forest wish to support are located at such a distance from the U.S. location of the Cordillera Club Foundation (the tax-exempt charitable sponsor) that the foundation might not want to take on the preservation campaign as a direct project. One of the other models probably will be more suitable.

LEAVING THE MODEL A NEST

The phenomenon of "leaving the nest" occurs mainly in the Model A situation, where the direct project has been established as an integral part of the sponsor. In all the other models, the project has a separate organizational identity and its own legal existence.

When a fiscal sponsor undertakes a direct project, it may be only temporary. It could be a brief period, while the project is awaiting IRS approval as a Section 501(c)(3) public charity. Or the incubation period could continue for several years while the project develops its program, administration, constituency and external resources.[5] Even if no separation is anticipated, it would be wise to give some thought to what would happen if the sponsor or the pro-

---

[5] For instance, Project Open Hand, a charity that provides meals to housebound persons with AIDS, was a direct project of the San Francisco Study Center for a year before it was separately incorporated in 1986.

ject leader eventually want to end the relationship. To not do so could prove disastrous.

While a direct project is part of its sponsor, all assets — including donations, grants, equipment purchased and other assets created by the project — belong to the sponsor. All employees and program results remain under the ultimate authority of the sponsor's board of directors, not the project personnel.

What provision should be made for the potential breakaway of a direct project? As soon as a project is taken on, the terms of a possible separation should be set forth in a board resolution adopted by the sponsor, in the sponsor's administrative procedures, or in a written contract. Following are some of the points that should be covered:

1. Identify the tangible assets connected to the project, including cash, equipment, supplies, inventory and other property. Even if a separate bank account is not used, fund accounting should be in place.

2. Identify intangible assets related to the project, such as its name, logo, any trademarks or copyrights, mailing lists, artistic rights, domain name, and any other intellectual property.

3. Identify the liabilities of the project, including any borrowed funds, unpaid bills, subscriptions to be filled, and the like.

4. Determine the preconditions for the sponsor to release the project. Does the project need to find another fiscal sponsor? Should the project be separately incorporated, with its 501(c)(3) tax-exemption and public charity status approved by the IRS? Should the project demonstrate its ability to operate competently on its own as a charity? Should the sponsor approve, or have a seat on, the project's board of directors? Should the consent of grantors, or creditors, be obtained?

5. Assuming preconditions have been met, identify who has the authority to decide that the project may leave. The project director? The sponsor's

> ## Without a plan
>
> The dispute between the Florida Audubon Society and its sponsored project, the Save the Manatee Club, illustrates what can happen when there is no plan for ending the project-sponsor relationship. *The Chronicle of Philanthropy*, August 11, 1992, reported that the breakup "shattered friendships, harmed reputations, distracted board members, and confused donors, while apparently setting back efforts to save one of Florida's most prominent and symbolic endangered species."

board? The sponsor's executive director? The project's advisory committee?

6. Determine the method of transferring assets and liabilities to the project. Usually, this is done by a grant from the sponsor to the new nonprofit entity created by the project, or it may be a grant from the old sponsor to a new sponsor if the project still does not have its own legal existence.

7. Provide for the enforceability of the terms of separation. This could be a bit tricky. If the sponsor wishes to maintain complete flexibility, the policy on separation can be stated in a board resolution or in procedures that the sponsor can modify at any time. If the project wants enforceable contract rights, but it has no separate legal standing, there must be some party with whom the sponsor can enter into a contract. Possibilities include:

- A sponsorship agreement with the project's advisory committee.
- An employment agreement with the project director.
- A grant agreement with one or more funders.
- An agreement with a board of directors set up for the project, pending IRS approval of the project's tax-exemption.

Finally, it is important to be clear that if no advance provision for "leaving the nest" is made, the sponsor has complete legal authority to insist that the direct project remain a part of the sponsor indefinitely. After all, the charitable donations and grants received to support the project are the property of the sponsor, and federal tax law requires that the sponsor exercise "discretion and control" over the use of those funds. The sponsor cannot relieve itself of this responsibility until it is satisfied that the sponsor's tax-exempt purposes will be furthered by granting the project's net assets to another nonprofit entity that will carry out the project's charitable mission.

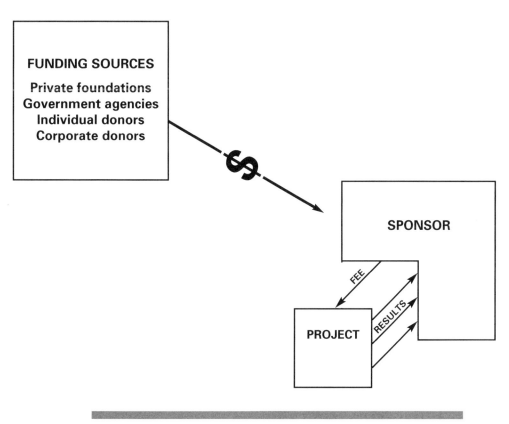

MODEL B — INDEPENDENT CONTRACTOR PROJECT

In Model B, the project belongs entirely to the sponsor, but the actual operation of the project is contracted out to a separate legal entity, which could be a person, a business firm, or some other type of organization. This arrangement differs from a grant (Model C), in that the sponsor wishes to maintain control over (and usually ownership of) the ultimate results of the project.

This model may be well-suited for some short-term projects, such as a book, play or film for which the project personnel are accustomed to producing a work of art on an independent contract. Among the hypothetical examples, Keith's film may be the best candidate for Model B if he is willing to share ownership with the Arts Consortium.

Contractor or employee?

The IRS has a multi-factor test for determining whether a person is properly classified as an independent contractor or must be treated as an employee. The main elements involve who has behavioral and financial control of the work and how the parties perceive their relationship. Some helpful sources are IRS Publication 1779, entitled "Independent Contractor or Employee…," and 15-A "Employer's Supplemental Tax Guide." If a sponsor misclassifies someone as an independent contractor who should have been treated as an employee, this may cause the IRS and state tax agencies to impose income taxes, Social Security taxes, disability taxes, and unemployment taxes (and penalties) on the employer. Misclassification also may expose the organization to workers' compensation claims, and the IRS or the state attorney general may impose personal liability on the corporate officers responsible for the misclassification.

Relationship

First, the sponsor must determine whether the people who will conduct the project can legally be classified (individually or collectively) as independent contractors. The sponsor could treat some project personnel as employees and others as independent contractors, but in the purest form of Model B, the entire project is contracted out to one person or entity. That person or entity must have its own legal, tax and accounting existence. It could be a sole proprietorship, a partnership, a business corporation, or even a nonprofit entity. Essentially, to contract independently with the sponsor, the project should be in business for itself, with its own letterhead, bank account, clientele and other attributes of separate existence.

The relationship between the sponsor and the project should be spelled out in a written contract. The agreement typically covers the work to be performed, the deadline, the amounts to be paid by the sponsor, the ownership of any property to be acquired or created, and the critical matter of who will bear various liabilities that may arise during the course of the project. It also makes plain that the independent contractor is responsible for income tax and payroll tax filings.

Handling of Charitable Donations

As in Model A, the project may take the leading role in raising funds in the name of the sponsor in order to support the project. All the same concerns exist — commitments may be made to donors that bind the sponsor, fundraising materials should be reviewed in advance, money raised must be treated as the sponsor's property, and restricted trust funds may be created by the solicitation process.

Administrative Charge

Like Model A, the sponsor may choose to allocate a portion of the funds raised to its general support, consistent with any commitments made to funders.

Liabilities

The extent and degree of liabilities for the sponsor will vary with the nature of the project, the terms of the contract, and the manner in which the project represents its connection to the sponsor in dealing with third parties.

Ownership

Property acquired or created by the project may belong to the sponsor or be shared with the project, depending on the terms of the contract. Care must be taken, however, when the sponsor is the sole source of funds for the project and valuable property is acquired or created with the sponsor's funds, yet some ownership rights are to remain with the project personnel as their personal or business assets. Depending on the facts and circumstances,[6] the IRS may view such an arrangement as conferring a substantial private benefit on a noncharitable beneficiary, which could jeopardize the sponsor's 501(c)(3) status. When intellectual property is involved, such as a copyright, unless the creator transfers ownership of the property to the sponsor, or it is co-owned by the project and sponsor, the courts may rule that the creator, as an independent contractor, still owns the copyright.[7]

---

[6] See, for example, IRS General Counsel Memorandum ("GCM") 39883.

[7] *Community for Creative Non-Violence v. James Earl Reid*, 490 U.S. 730, 109 S. Ct. 2166, 104 L. Ed. 2d 811 (1989).

Tax Reporting

The contract payments made by the sponsor appear on its IRS Form 990 tax return. In addition, if the project is a sole proprietorship or partnership, the sponsor should issue a Form 1099 to the project for the amount of funds disbursed during the year.[8] The type of tax return filed by the project depends on its legal status. If it is a sole proprietorship, one person reports the project income and expenses on his or her Form 1040, Schedules C and SE. Partnerships and corporations have their own tax returns to file. Whatever the business form of the project, the project early on must determine whether the other people working on the project are its partners, employees or independent contractors, and comply with its tax-reporting obligations accordingly.

APPLYING MODEL B TO THE HYPOTHETICALS

#1 — The Artists

In the field of art, an independent contractor arrangement is sometimes the best, particularly where the artist has experience running his or her own business, has other clients, and where the sponsor wants to acquire the end product as part of its general program. Here, the artists could form a partnership to make the film, or they could incorporate, or Keith could be sole proprietor of the project. (The sponsor could even provide technical assistance to help establish and manage this venture under Model F.)

Assuming Keith acts as a sole proprietor filmmaker, the contract between Keith and the Arts Consortium would provide for the consortium to pay a flat $100,000 fee to him (perhaps in staged installments), out of which Keith would pay for the personnel costs and other expenses. If the film goes over budget, Keith is still obligated to finish the film, even if he has to borrow,

---

[8] See the IRS instructions for Form 1099 to determine when and how the reporting form must be used. If the project is incorporated, Form 1099 is not required.

---

do more fund raising or pay out of his own pocket to do it. All liabilities would be borne by Keith, not the consortium. At the end, Keith typically would assign copyright in the film to the consortium. However, other ownership arrangements are possible. For instance, the consortium could acquire a set number of copies of the film and exclusive distribution rights for the first year, reserving all other rights to Keith, so long as the agreement serves the consortium's charitable purposes and does not result in an unreasonable or excessive private benefit to Keith. In any event, matters of liability and ownership must be thoroughly negotiated and stated in writing in advance, to prevent disputes from arising between artist and sponsor that could destroy the project.

> **Film projects and taxes**
>
> Resolving the issue of ownership may be heavily influenced by the artist's tax situation. Filmmakers who own the films they produce have been subject to uniform capitalization rules that may cause the sponsor's entire payment to be taxable income. However, new tax code section 181, valid until 2009, may give the filmmaker tax relief by allowing all costs to be deducted. We strongly recommend that filmmakers get good legal and accounting advice.

Model B probably would not be a good choice for the incubation of Amparo's dance troupe; that would require her to establish and administer a separate legal entity before she is ready to do so.

#2 — The Human Services Project

Model B might solve part of Angel Island Community Church's difficulties administering the hospice. A new, independent entity (assume it is for-profit) could be formed to receive the assets and liabilities of the hospice and to manage the project under a contract with the church. If the church determines that its charitable purposes are better served by transferring the project to a for-profit entity, and the new owners pay fair market value for the net assets (if any) of the hospice, the transfer would be proper. The church could keep the care contract with the village government and subcontract with the hospice organization, if it wished to keep the hospice project as a community program within its ultimate control. If former church/hospice personnel are the owners of the new entity, the transaction should be structured carefully to avoid any improper inurement or private benefit to the new owners.

Alternatively, the independent for-profit hospice could contract directly with the village and eliminate the church's middle position. However, tax-deductible gifts and bequests would still have to be paid to the church because the hospice would not be a 501(c)(3) organization. The church could continue to fund the hospice, in accordance with the wishes of the donors, through a series of grants (see Model C), even though the hospice has become a for-profit entity, if the church determines that would serve its charitable purposes.

#3 — The Environmental Group

Again, considering the distance involved, the Cordillera Club Foundation would probably not want the preservation project to be an integral part of its programs, and would opt to fund the project with one or more grants (see Model C) rather than through some kind of independent service contract with FBRF or the local Brazilian community organization.

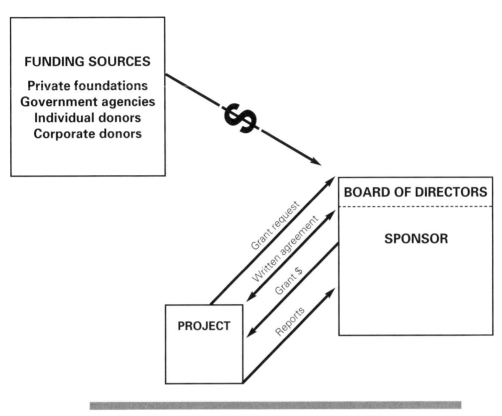

FUNDING SOURCES

Private foundations
Government agencies
Individual donors
Corporate donors

BOARD OF DIRECTORS

SPONSOR

Grant request

Written agreement

Grant $

Reports

PROJECT

MODEL C — PREAPPROVED GRANT RELATIONSHIP

Model C is a very widespread, and widely misunderstood, form of fiscal sponsorship. Often, the sponsor and project are not aware that they have created a grantor-grantee relationship between them. The project may put a lot of energy into a grant request presented to the funding source in the name of the sponsor, to which the grant is then awarded. The sponsor disburses funds to the project, and everybody tends to see that grant as the only one. Actually, there are two levels of grant relationship that occur, which is why some people refer to this model as "regranting." As we will show, it is best if the sponsor and project create their own grantor-grantee relationship before the funding source is approached.

If there is a "trap for the unwary" among fiscal sponsorship arrangements, Model C is it. If the control mechanisms are not administered properly, Model C can collapse into a "conduit" or "step transaction" in which the IRS will disregard the role of the sponsor and declare that the funding source has, in effect, made a payment directly to a non-501(c)(3) project. For funding sources, the result will be that the donor cannot take a charitable deduction, or that the private foundation must now observe the strictures of "expenditure responsibility." The project will find that its funding has disappeared. The sponsor may lose its tax-exempt status for failure to exercise sufficient control over its funds, permitting those funds to be used in a noncharitable manner.

As a high-ranking IRS official observed in a conversation with the author, depending on how Model C is applied, it could be the basis for anything from a bona fide tax plan to a case of criminal tax fraud. The IRS would treat very harshly any use of a 501(c)(3) sponsor to "launder" money where the donor is trying to get a charitable deduction for his or her own personal, business, political, or other nondeductible expenditures.

Model C is cousin to another three-party funding arrangement called the "donor-advised fund," where a donor makes contributions to a public charity, such as a community foundation, with the understanding that the donor may recommend, from time to time, other organizations to receive certain amounts as grants from the donor's fund. For this arrangement to avoid being declared a conduit by the IRS, the donor's choice of grantees must be treated as nonbinding advice to the charity.[9]

---

[9] Although commonly used in the charitable sector, the term "donor-advised fund" is not found in the Internal Revenue Code or in Treasury Regulations. Good articles on this phenomenon are "The Emergence of the Donor-Advised Fund," by Victoria Bjorklund, *Paul Streckfus' EO Tax Journal*, May 1998, page 15, and Rodriguez, Choi and Mittermaier, "The Tax-Exempt Status of Commercially Sponsored Donor-Advised Funds," 17 *Exempt Organizations Tax Review* 95 (July 1997). While fiscal sponsorship tends to be a service to projects, donor-advised funds are seen as a service to donors, and grantees typically have their own 501(c)(3) status. Some community foundations and others have been known to use their donor-advised fund accounts to make Model C regrants, but often the mechanism doesn't quite fit the sponsorship situation. At any time, Congress may enact new tax rules for donor-advised funds, which may or may not affect fiscal sponsorships.

As we shall see, Model C is best suited to the hypothetical situation of the Friends of the Brazilian Rain Forest, where the Cordillera Club Foundation could serve as fiscal sponsor and make a grant for charitable purposes to a noncharitable U.S. organization such as FBRF, or to a foreign organization. However, Model C could be used in any situation where the sponsor is willing to carefully administer a grant system and the project is willing to shoulder the responsibilities of independent legal existence, whether it is for an environmental, human service, cultural, or other charitable cause.

A close call

In one of the few IRS ratings that refer to nonprofit "fiscal agency," Technical Advice Memorandum 8936002, a 501(c)(3) organization almost lost its tax-exempt status for activities by its sponsored projects that came very close to political intervention during the 1984 presidential election campaign.

Relationship

In Model C, the project does not become a program belonging to the sponsor. Instead, the sponsor chooses to further its exempt purposes **indirectly**, by giving financial support to another entity or person for a specific project that the sponsor has reason to believe will advance the sponsor's charitable goals. This is a classic grant relationship.[10] Unlike an independent contractor relationship, the sponsor is not seeking ownership of any part of the results of the work, but simply an assurance that the project will use the grant funds in a reasonable effort to accomplish the ends described in the grant proposal.

A properly administered Model C grant relationship proceeds in steps (the documents needed are in **bold type**):

Step 1: The person or organization that wants to do the project presents a written **grant request** to the sponsor, describing a specific program to be conducted.

Step 2: The sponsor evaluates the grant proposal to determine whether the project is charitable and carries out the sponsor's tax-exempt purposes.

Step 3: The sponsor's board of directors reviews and approves the project as furthering the sponsor's exempt purposes. In a **board resolution**, the sponsor states its conclusions and approves a grant to the project, to be funded

---

[10] Rev. Rul. 68-489, 1968-2 C.B. 210.

to a certain amount, or to the extent that the sponsor receives outside funds for the project. Thus, before funds are solicited from donors, foundations, or government agencies, the sponsor has preapproved the project as its grantee. It is important that the project be approved or ratified ultimately at the board level rather than merely by staff.

Step 4: The sponsor and the project sign a written **grant agreement** [11] setting forth all the terms and conditions that apply to the project's use of the grant and relations with funding sources. The specific work to be performed by the project using grant funds should be spelled out in the grant agreement, in a cover letter, or by reference to the written project proposal.

Step 5: The project, the sponsor, or some combination of the two, solicits funds for the specific grant to be made by the sponsor to the project. The sponsor's **bylaws** provide that such solicitations shall be made only on the condition that the sponsor retains complete control and discretion over the use of all contributions it receives. That element of sponsor discretion and control should be made known, in writing, to the funding sources.

Step 6: As the sponsor receives donations and grants for the specific project, the money is taken into income by the sponsor and then disbursed as grant payments to the person or organization conducting the project, subject to the terms of the grant agreement.

Step 7: The project makes periodic **written reports** to the sponsor, in accordance with the grant agreement, showing its actual expenditures of grant funds and its progress toward accomplishing the purposes of the grant.

It is important to understand that, like the independent contractor, a project under Model C has its own legal, tax and accounting identity. The project could belong to an individual (as a sole proprietor) or to a nonprofit organization of some kind other than a 501(c)(3). It also could be a partnership or a business corporation.

Occasionally, the project is an informal group of people who do not plan to incorporate. The project must, however, declare what kind of entity it is when it opens a bank account. The bank will ask for a federal employer

---

[11] See the Appendix for a sample Model C grant agreement.

identification number (FEIN) or someone's
Social Security number. The sponsor's FEIN
should not be used, because to do so would indicate that the project is an integral legal part of the
sponsor. Likewise, it is not a good idea to use a
person's Social Security number for a project that
is a group effort because that person may be
treated as the legal owner of the funds in the
account. It is best, usually, for an informal project
to apply for its own FEIN by filling out a simple,
one-page IRS Form SS-4, identifying itself as an
"unincorporated association" on the form. If a
project is in a hurry to open a bank account, it can call the IRS and obtain the
FEIN over the telephone or online at www.irs.gov.

> ## Projects are legal entities
>
> The Model C project should not lapse into a false sense of security because it has a sponsor. The project, not the sponsor, is responsible for the project's tax returns, employment taxes, insurance, debts, liabilities and other legal obligations.

Handling of Charitable Donations

As in Models A and B, the project may take the leading role in raising
funds for the project in the name of the sponsor. Again, care is needed because
commitments may be made to donors that bind the sponsor. Fund-raising
materials should be reviewed in advance, money raised must be treated as the
sponsor's own revenues, and restricted trust funds may be created by the solicitation process.

When funds are granted to a non-501(c)(3) project, the IRS requires
the sponsor to maintain full discretion and control over the funds received for
the project. Donors relinquish all control over the funds once they are given to
the sponsor. The sponsor may not be legally obligated to fund the project, and
the sponsor may have the right to withdraw financial support from the project
and redirect the funds to another purpose, in which case the donor may have
no legal recourse against the sponsor.[12]

Ordinarily, however, the funds for a preapproved grant are solicited for
a particular purpose. Funders would naturally expect the sponsor of a preapproved project to fund the project so long as the project follows its grant

---

[12] This is the fact pattern in the *National Foundation* case cited in footnote 2.

---

agreement. For instance, the terms of a government grant to a sponsor might provide that the funds are to be spent for a specific work of art to be created or film to be produced, with the funds to be returned to the government agency if the project fails. Similarly, if a project has been adhering to its grant agreement with a sponsor and the sponsor is holding back funds for the project, the project should be able to enforce the grant agreement as a contractual obligation of the sponsor to pay. Also, the state attorney general may insist that charitable funds raised for a particular purpose be held in trust for that purpose, and not allow the sponsor to divert them to another project.

So there is an apparent contradiction between federal tax law, which emphasizes the discretion of the sponsor, and state charitable trust law, which emphasizes commitments made to donors. There are two solutions:

1. *The Unrestricted Fund.* Under this option, great care is taken not to make or imply any commitments to funding sources. The solicitation materials and grant agreement with the project make plain that the sponsor, in its sole discretion, may withdraw support from the project and spend funds for some other purpose within its overall charitable purposes. If these steps are taken, federal tax law requirements are easily met and the charitable trust problem is avoided.

2. *The Restricted Fund.* The act of preapproval, plus a carefully drafted grant agreement creating a restricted fund, should satisfy the IRS,[13] the funder, the project and the attorney general. Preapproval means that the sponsor has already exercised, at the outset, discretion and control over the funds to be raised by declaring that financial support of the project will further its exempt purposes. What remains to be spelled out in the grant agreement are (1) performance requirements for the project, (2) the right of the sponsor to withhold, withdraw, and demand return of the grant funds if the performance requirements (or other conditions affecting the sponsor) are not met, and, in that circumstance, (3) the right of the sponsor to redirect grant funds to some

---

[13] This process has been confirmed by the IRS as an appropriate mechanism for fiscal sponsorship arrangements in the context of U.S. charities soliciting donations that will then be used for grants to foreign organizations. Rev. Rul. 66-79, 1966-1 C.B. 48, reproduced in the Appendix.

other person or entity who can complete the project.[14] The restricted fund, even though it is committed to a particular project, should pass muster with the IRS because the sponsor retains the right to choose other people to do the project if the individuals originally involved with the project do not perform.

Administrative Charge

As in Models A and B, the sponsor may establish a charge for general administration, overhead and fund raising, so long as this does not contravene any agreements made with grantors or donors. In some situations, such as government grants, the amount of this overhead charge must be negotiated with and approved by the funding source. The charge can be a fixed dollar amount, but more commonly it is set at a certain percentage of the funds raised for the project. In actuality, the sponsor is not charging the project a fee; the sponsor is simply retaining a certain portion of funds which are the sponsor's property anyway. The administrative charge should be specified in the grant agreement. There is no normal or customary percentage, and so far there is no federal tax law declaring any type or amount of charge to be improper.[15] The amount of the charge is a matter of negotiation.

Liabilities

The liabilities of the grantor generally are quite limited in a grantor-grantee relationship. The grantee does not act as the agent of the grantor legal-

---

[14] If no one else can finish the project, the law of *cy pres* requires the sponsor to use the funds in a manner that will accomplish the donor's intentions as nearly as possible. If the funds originally came from a government agency or private foundation grant, that contract or grant agreement may dictate the final disposition of funds.

[15] In the *National Foundation* case cited in footnote 2, the IRS argued that a 2.5% charge for administrative costs indicated that the organization was really a commercial enterprise serving a collection of clients. The court rejected this argument, noting that "every organization bears some operating expense" and that the amount of any contribution available for the intended charitable project would not be diminished by more than 2.5%. The implication is that the lower the charge, the less likely it is to be controversial. (National Foundation also charged 8.5% of the first $500 contribution for administrative and fund-raising costs.)

ly,[16] so any obligations incurred, damages or injuries caused, or misconduct committed by the grantee, should not be the responsibility of the sponsor. The main liabilities of the sponsor flow from the grantor's obligations under tax law to maintain discretion and control over use of the grant funds, and from the terms of any grant agreement between the sponsor and the private foundation or government agency that originally provided the funds. Basically, the sponsor is liable only for properly selecting and paying the grantee, and for reasonably monitoring the grant to make sure the funds are spent in accordance with the grant agreement.

However, despite the limited role of a sponsor as a grantor under Model C, many conscientious sponsors find that a certain degree of supervision and assistance (see Model F) is necessary to help grantees succeed with a charitable project.

Charitable vs. commercial activities

The IRS distinguishes artistic activities that are charitable from those that are commercial by examining the facts and circumstances motivating the grantor and grantee. A pair of 1966 rulings illustrate how the line is drawn. In Rev. Rul. 66-103, 1966-1 C.B. 134, the IRS approved the charitable status of an organization making grants to writers, composers, painters, sculptors and scholars, where (1) the grantees "would not otherwise be able to undertake or finish [the projects] due to the lack of funds," (2) "preference is given to persons showing distinction or promise in their respective fields," (3) the grantees "promise to make their work available for the benefit of the public in ways customary and appropriate to the particular work," and (4) "the purpose of such grants is to assist the recipient to carry on his creative efforts." The grants were unconditional in that the grantee retained all rights to the work created, and the grantor organization derived no monetary benefit from the work. By contrast, in Rev. Rul. 66-104, 1966-1 C.B. 135, the IRS disapproved charitable status for an organization set up to pay writers to prepare economics textbooks, where the works were sold to commercial publishers and royalties were split between the organization and the writers. The IRS found this to be "an enterprise conducted in an essentially commercial manner, in which all the participants expect to receive a monetary return."

---

[16] That is to say, the grantee is not acting as an agent of the sponsor as a recipient of a grant. However, during the earlier fund-raising stage, the project may have acted as an agent of the sponsor as a solicitor of funds, creating liabilities for the sponsor.

Ownership

A grant, like a gift, is given because the grantor is sympathetic to and supports the work of the grantee, not because the grantor is expecting something of financial benefit in return. Therefore, if anything of tangible or intangible value is created with the aid of the grant, it generally remains the property of the grantee. In the fields of art, film and music, the IRS has recognized that the creator may financially benefit from the use of charitable funds. This is not improper. The benefit to the artist personally is an incidental result of expenditures to promote the arts. This is perfectly appropriate if the artist is within the charitable class of recipients.

In the preapproved grant model, the end result of the project, if any, is owned by the project. This helps protect the sponsor from liability, because the property is created by the project on its own behalf, not on behalf of the sponsor, and so the project is not the agent of the sponsor.

This does not prevent the sponsor from stipulating that, under certain conditions, the grant is to be partially or wholly repaid from the net proceeds of sale, rental, distribution or other exploitation of the asset created. However, the repayment should be capped at the amount of the grant, unless the sponsor wishes to be in the position of a part-owner or a business co-venturer with the grantee. No law requires that the sponsor be repaid or reimbursed, however. It is left to negotiation between the sponsor and the project.

Tax Reporting

The grant payments made by the sponsor appear on its IRS Form 990 tax return.[17] Unlike the independent contractor situation, the sponsor is generally not required to issue an IRS Form 1099 to the project.[18] In some cases, particularly where the grantee is a foreign individual, the sponsor may have to

---

[17] As a grantee, the project's name and address must be listed on a schedule required by Part II, Line 22, of Form 990. If the grantee is not a 501(c)(3) organization, the grant must be reported also on Line 51, Part VII, of Schedule A to Form 990.

[18] There are exceptions: Certain federal grants are taxable, and should be reported on Form 1099-G. Prizes and awards may be taxable, and if so, they are reported on Form 1099-MISC. Some scholarship and fellowship grants are taxable, and reporting on Form W-2 may be required.

withhold for U.S. income taxes. A charitable grant may or may not be taxable income to the project.[19] The type of tax return filed by the project depends on its legal status. If it is a sole proprietorship and the grant is taxable, the owner reports the project income and expenses on his or her Form 1040, Schedules C and SE. Business partnerships and corporations have their own tax returns to file. If the project is a nonprofit organization, it will need to file a Form 990 if its annual income is normally more than $25,000.[20] Whatever the legal form of the project, the project also has to determine whether the other people working on the project are its partners, employees, or independent contractors, and comply with its tax reporting obligations accordingly.

APPLYING MODEL C TO THE HYPOTHETICALS

#1 — The Artists

Model C grant arrangements are frequently used in the field of art, where so many artists, musicians, filmmakers, choreographers, writers and others have small, struggling enterprises that need charitable financial support.[21] Few are in a position to set up or administer a 501(c)(3) public charity that could directly receive deductible contributions, so many seek a fiscal sponsor. Although Model A provides the most security for the project and the most control for the sponsor, many prefer the independence of Model C.

In this hypothetical, Model C would not be the best incubator for Amparo's dance troupe; she would be better off as a direct project of the consortium until she can form a free-standing nonprofit organization. However, Model C is a viable option for Keith's film.

---

[19] To completely analyze the taxability of various forms of grants would be beyond the scope of this book, even though this issue is often critical to the choice of fiscal sponsorship method. See Appendix, Commentary on Taxability of Grants.

[20] "Normally," in the first year of operation, is interpreted to mean under $37,500, according to the Form 990 instructions.

[21] Film Arts Foundation has supported hundreds of documentary films, including a number of Academy Award nominees and winners, using fiscal sponsorship.

Before applying for a preapproved grant from the consortium, Keith needs to decide what the legal form of his project will be. As in Model B, Keith and Amparo could form a partnership to make the film, or form a corporation, or Keith could be sole proprietor of the project, perhaps with technical assistance from the sponsor (Model F). The project entity, whatever it is, should have a bank account separate from the sponsor and separate from the personal accounts of the artists.

Sometimes, projects try to avoid setting up a business form by having the sponsor pay the costs of the project directly, including their own compensation. While it is possible for a sponsor to disburse a grant in this fashion, it tends to blur the boundaries between the sponsor and the project, and could result in the arrangement being treated as an employee or independent contractor program, which increases the liability exposure for the sponsor. If the sponsor wants to avoid that potential liability, it would be best to have a written agreement making plain that the arrangement is between grantor and grantee. If the sponsor does not want to pay the grant in a lump sum, staged payments triggered when the project reaches certain performance benchmarks are more consistent with the concept of a grant.

Once the artists are clear on the legal form of the film project entity, the sponsorship should follow the seven-step process outlined previously. Because the prospective funding sources include government agencies and private foundations, the restricted fund option probably would be most suitable.

The 10% administrative charge, if it is reasonable and does not exceed the project's share of the sponsor's overhead costs, and so long as no agreement with any funding source is violated, would be appropriate.

Unless otherwise stated in the grant agreement, Keith (assuming he is a sole proprietor) will own the film and all the rights created or acquired during the course of making the film.[22] However, the consortium wants the grant to be repaid if the film makes a profit. The consortium may want to specify the manner of distribution of the film, as well. Sometimes, especially with govern-

---

[22] For some artists, such as filmmakers, a decision on ownership affects the tax situation of the project entity. As mentioned in the discussion of independent contractor arrangements, if the grant is deemed taxable income for the artist, capitalization rules may place an unacceptable tax burden upon the artist.

ment grants for films, the funder's contract with the sponsor imposes many requirements for government approval of distribution, notification of personnel changes, payback to the government, ownership of copyright, permissible overhead charges, and elaborate financial reports. These are legal obligations of the sponsor, the grant agreement should make clear that the project will perform all those conditions, and should specify who will bear the expense of compliance.

#2 — The Human Services Project

As in Model B, use of Model C to support the hospice assumes that the hospice establishes itself as an independent legal entity and properly receives the hospice assets and liabilities formerly belonging to the church. The grant model further assumes that the hospice is no longer part of the church's direct program, and that the hospice has its own care contract with the village government. The remaining relationship of the church to the hospice, then, involves the handling of tax-deductible gifts, grants, contributions and bequests.

> ### Repaying a grant
>
> If a grant is to be repaid, the contingent repayment provisions must specify which expenditures, e.g. deferred compensation for the filmmakers, are allowable before a profit is declared. Also, there is a variety of ways to structure the repayment, such as the order in which various funders will be paid, each funder's percentage share, and whether the sponsor's share will be capped.

The seven-step, preapproved grant process is the same for the hospice and the church as it is for Keith and the consortium. As the prospective funders are mainly individual donors, the grant relationship could be set up either as a restricted fund, or, if donors would accept the chance that their gifts might be spent for other purposes of the church, as an unrestricted fund.

The hypothetical also presents the question as to whether friends or family of patients at the hospice can make a tax-deductible charitable contribution to the church to help pay the high cost of medicine for a specific patient. Federal tax law requires that the beneficiaries of a charitable contribution be indefinite.[23] The Tax Court has held that payments to give special

---

[23] *Russell v. Allen*, 107 U.S. 163, 2 S.Ct. 327, 27 L.Ed. 397 (1883).

advantages to a particular child who was being cared for in a children's home were not deductible when earmarked for the benefit of that child.[24] Individual benefit may be proper, however, if that person is a member of a charitable class. For example, suppose the church set up a medications fund for the hospice, to which patients could apply for financial assistance. If a particular patient applied and was preapproved, then anyone, including his or her friends and family, could make deductible donations to that fund. The church would, of course, maintain the right to independently select the patients who would receive, or continue to receive, financial assistance regardless whether the funds came from a friend or relative. If the precise details of this process are not observed, the IRS could treat the donation as nondeductible.

#3 — The Environmental Group

Holly, the Friends of the Brazilian Rain Forest, and the Cordillera Club Foundation will probably find that the preapproved grant model suits them best. To start the Model C seven-step process, FBRF makes a grant proposal to the Cordillera Club Foundation. When the foundation board of directors reviews and approves the grant, it should decide whether to take the restricted or unrestricted fund approach. Typically, the grant proposal would have a budget indicating the amounts to be spent on litigation, lobbying, and support of the local native community organization. The part designated for the Brazilian group can be paid through FBRF, or directly to the Brazilian group, since the IRS has recognized the preapproved grant process as an acceptable method to raise money in the United States for the support of foreign organizations.

What about the possibility that Holly may have a business interest in the rain forest area that is being preserved, considering that her herbal tea

> ## Lobbying
>
> The 501(c)(3) sponsor's lobbying activity cannot be substantial. The portion of the grant allocated for lobbying will need to be reported by the sponsor on Schedule A of its IRS Form 990 as an expenditure in some detail. Or, if the sponsor elects the lobbying expenditure test under §501(h), which establishes percentage limitations, the amount can be combined with any other lobbying expenditures made by the sponsor and reported on Schedule A.

---

[24] *S.E. Thomason v. Commissioner*, 2 T.C. 441 (1943).

---

company receives most of certain of its herbs from that region? To be a charitable contribution, a donation has to be a gift, motivated by "detached and disinterested generosity," not by the expectation of receiving a valuable benefit in return. Depending on the precise facts, however, Holly's benefit from the preservation activity could be so incidental and tangential that any IRS challenge to the validity of the charitable deduction would be very unlikely.[25]

On the other hand, environmental preservation efforts occasionally are initiated and primarily funded by a few neighboring property owners who have a direct financial interest in the outcome. Care must be taken in the formation of the action group and in the sponsorship arrangement to prevent domination or control by the owners of adjacent or nearby land. An improper private benefit could jeopardize not only their deductions, but the charitable nature of the project and even the 501(c)(3) status of the sponsor.[26]

As for the Mormon missionary, Model X (see Appendix) describes a method approved by the U.S. Supreme Court for parents to support their missionary children with deductible contributions. However, Model C can work, too. The missionary could prepare a grant request, which would be submitted either to the Mormon church or to the foundation as fiscal sponsor and, if approved, the parents and anyone else could make deductible contributions to

---

[25] In *Commissioner v. Duberstein*, 363 U.S. 278 (1960), the U.S. Supreme Court determined that a purported gift of a car from one business associate to another would not be treated as a "gift" for tax purposes because it was not motivated by "detached and disinterested generosity." The court determined that the donor expected to receive some direct or indirect business benefits from making this gift. In *Ottawa Silicia v. U.S.*, 699 F.2d 1124, (Fed. Cir. 1983), the federal Circuit Court of Appeals agreed with the IRS that a corporation that mined sand should not be entitled to a charitable contribution deduction for its contribution of 49 acres of land to a local school district. In that case, the donor expected to receive access to roads constructed by the school district on the donated land as a result of the contribution. In *Singer v. U.S.*, 449 F.2d 413 (Ct.Cl. 1972), the Supreme Court allowed a charitable deduction where the return benefit from the contribution of sewing machines to charities was merely favorable public image, but it denied a deduction where Singer contributed machines to exempt organizations that trained students how to sew because, the court determined, Singer made such contributions in anticipation of increased sales. See also Rev. Rul. 80-77, 1980-1 C.B. 56 (contribution to Girl Scouts deductible even though donor's daughter was a member — minimal benefit). Rev. Rul. 83-104, 1983-2 C.B. 46 (contributions to private schools attended by donor's children — circumstances under which deductible); Rev. Rul. 69-90, 1969-1 C.B. 63 (merchants and property owners could deduct contributions to city to acquire public parking that would only indirectly benefit merchants).

the church or foundation to fund the grant. However, as with the hospice medications fund, proper administration of the fund is critical. The sponsor must retain complete control, that is, the independent right to select and to change the recipient of the financial support.

---

[26] See, e.g., *Ginsberg v. Commissioner* 46 T.C. 47 (1966) (association formed to dredge waterways held nonexempt because it conveyed a substantial private benefit to owners of property who lived adjacent to waterway and who were the principal contributors to the association). See also *Westward Ho v. Commissioner* T.C. Memo 1992-192, 63 TCM 2617 (an association formed to relocate homeless individuals held not to be exempt because it was formed by and primarily benefited the town merchants who were the primary contributors and whose businesses served to benefit); Rev. Rul. 75-286, 1975-2 C.B. 210, (nonprofit organization with membership limited to the residents and merchants within a city block was formed to preserve and beautify the public areas in the block, thereby benefiting the public but also providing a substantial benefit to the members' property and, therefore, did not qualify for exemption under Section 501(c)(3)).

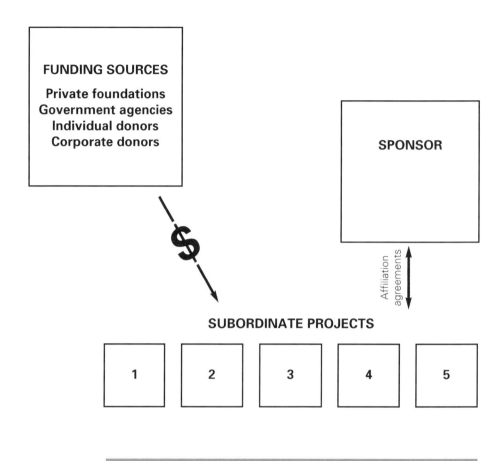

FUNDING SOURCES

Private foundations
Government agencies
Individual donors
Corporate donors

SPONSOR

Affiliation agreements

SUBORDINATE PROJECTS

| 1 | 2 | 3 | 4 | 5 |

MODEL D — GROUP EXEMPTION

Typically, a project seeks a sponsor because the project does not have its own 501(c)(3) tax exemption. Obtaining 501(c)(3) tax status can be a lengthy and costly process during which the project must respond to a battery of IRS questions to demonstrate that its purposes, governing structure, operations and budget all meet IRS requirements. For a small or short-term project, the application process might not be feasible.

Although it is not widely known, the IRS has had for decades a procedure whereby certain organizations can receive 501(c)(3) tax status without applying to the IRS. The "group exemption" process, set forth in a simple, three-page IRS Revenue Procedure,[27] is designed for "subordinate organizations that are affiliated with and under the general supervision or control of a central organization."

In a nutshell, the central 501(c)(3) organization applies to the IRS for a group exemption letter covering its subordinates, attesting that each of the subordinates is also qualified under 501(c)(3). After the initial group exemption letter is issued, subordinates can be deleted or added to an annual listing that the central organization files with the IRS at least 90 days before the end of its fiscal year.

A central organization is defined as an organization that has one or more subordinates under its general supervision or control. A subordinate is defined as a chapter, local, post, or unit of a central organization.

The group exemption process is mainly used by nonprofits that are geographically organized on a state, regional or national basis. The Roman Catholic Church in the United States is a prime example. However, there is no reason why a sponsor (the central organization) should not be able to obtain a group exemption letter covering a variety of artistic, community, environmental, or other charitable projects (subordinate units) if the arrangement meets the IRS tests for affiliation and supervision or control.

Model D is a good alternative to Model C for ongoing projects that wish to have a permanent, yet independent, affiliation with the sponsor. Amparo's dance troupe might fit this description. Because the Model D project can directly receive charitable donations, there is less exposure to IRS concerns that the sponsor is acting as a conduit.

Relationship

The key elements of the relationship between a sponsor and its subordinate projects that need to be demonstrated to the IRS for a group exemption are:

---

[27] Rev. Proc. 80-27, 1980-1 C.B. 677. At some point, the IRS may issue a revised Revenue Procedure for group rulings to replace Rev. Proc. 80-27. See also IRS Publication No. 557, "Tax-Exempt Status for Your Organization."

- The projects must be affiliated with the sponsor.
- The projects must be subject to the general supervision or control of the sponsor.
- The sponsor must establish that the projects are all exempt under 501(c)(3), and attest that they are not private foundations.
- Each project must authorize the sponsor, in writing, to include it in the group exemption letter.
- Projects must adopt uniform governing instruments prescribed by the sponsor, or use governing documents that show the requisite subordinate relationship.
- The sponsor must present a detailed description of the purposes and activities of the projects, including the sources of receipts and the nature of expenditures. The description must be affirmed and signed by a principal officer of the sponsor, to the best of his or her knowledge.
- The sponsor, and each of the projects, must have separate federal employer identification numbers (FEINs), as they are separate legal entities.

> ## Project as public charity
>
> The sponsor has the duty to ensure that each of the projects is a qualified public charity, so the project does not need to obtain an advance ruling from the IRS, nor is it required to supply public support data to the IRS. Oversight is shifted from the IRS to the sponsor, so the sponsor should have some way of determining that each project has sufficiently diversified sources of support, or some other basis for classification as a public charity.

The last point is worth special emphasis. The project's relationship with the sponsor relieves the project of the need to apply for its own 501(c)(3) exemption, but it does not remove any other aspect or obligation of the project's separate existence. The project may be, and often is, an unincorporated association. To help protect the sponsor from liability, however, it may be advisable to incorporate the project as a nonprofit corporation in the state where it is located. The state may require the project to file a separate income tax or property tax exemption application. The project has its own legal, tax and accounting identity as a nonprofit organization. The IRS can audit any particular project and revoke its 501(c)(3) exemption, leaving the rest of the projects and the sponsor unaffected.

The terms of the project's affiliation with the sponsor should be spelled out in a written agreement that includes items such as permission for the project to use the sponsor's trademarks (if appropriate), the respective liabilities of the sponsor and the project, the scope of the project's work, financial account-ability, affairs of the project over which the sponsor wishes to exert authority, and the process for the sponsor to follow if the affiliate status of a project is to be suspended or terminated.

Handling of Charitable Donations

Having obtained its own 501(c)(3) status by way of the group exemp-tion, a Model D project can seek grants and raise funds in its own name, using the group exemption letter of the sponsor. The sponsor does not have to han-dle any funds for the project.

This makes it easy for the project to raise money, but it may create a sit-uation in which the projects compete with the sponsor, or with each other, for funding from the same sources. The sponsor can reduce the likelihood of com-petition by providing in the affiliation agreement that a project must coordi-nate its fund raising with the sponsor, or even that a project's grant requests or fund-raising campaigns must be cleared in advance by the sponsor.

Administrative Charge

Unless the sponsor insists that all projects must route their fund-raising revenues through the sponsor, the sponsor will not be able to deduct an administrative fee or percentage from funds in its possession while in transit. However, there is nothing objectionable about the sponsor imposing dues or some sort of affiliation fee upon the projects under Model D, to compensate the sponsor for the benefits provided to the project. This could be a flat monthly or annual charge, or determined on a sliding scale according to the amount of the project's revenues.

Liabilities

The extent of a parent sponsor's liability for the acts or omissions of its subordinate affiliates is a subject that arises occasionally concerning organiza-tions such as lodges and chapters, unions and locals, national churches and local congregations. Generally speaking, each affiliate is separately liable for its own torts and contracts, unless the parent takes some affirmative act (such as guaranteeing a loan or co-sponsoring an event) of responsibility for the affiliate's obligation. Liability problems under Model D can be prevented, for the most part, by separate incorporation and by a carefully drafted affiliation agreement which stipulates that the project does not and shall not act as an agent for the sponsor unless specifically authorized to do so. Again, the manner in which the project represents its connection to the sponsor in dealing with third parties is important.

Ownership

The Model D project, rather than the sponsor, is the sole owner of any assets that it accumulates or creates in the course of its work, unless the affiliation agreement states otherwise. Some sponsors may require that legal title to project bank accounts and property be held "in trust for" the sponsor, so that the sponsor can quickly take over the project's assets if the project goes astray. Most commonly, the project's articles of incorporation are required to state that the net assets of the project will become the property of the sponsor in the event that the project is dissolved.

Tax Reporting

There are basically two choices for a project's federal tax reporting under the Model D group exemption. Either information about the project may be included in a group return filed by the sponsor on behalf of two or more of its projects, or the project may file its own separate return. In either case, the sponsor must file its own return separate from the group return.[28]

IRS Form 990 is used no matter which filing approach is taken. Projects with revenues normally less than $25,000 per year do not need to file their own returns, nor do they need to be included in a group return. In most cases, the sponsor will prefer that projects be responsible for their own filings, but for projects incapable of doing so, the sponsor may gather financial data from such projects and combine it in a group return as a service to its affiliates. All projects included in a group return must have the same fiscal year as the sponsor.

[28] For more information on group tax returns, see Treasury Regulations Section 1.6033.2(d), IRS Publication No. 557, "Tax-Exempt Status for Your Organization," and IRS Instructions for Form 990, Instruction R.

In most cases, each project must meet the same public support test as the sponsor under a group exemption, to maintain public charity status, so projects need to make sure they have a sufficient mix of public funds in their revenue base to qualify. Some projects may qualify as public charities without diverse sources of support.[29]

There is another annual IRS filing unique to group exemptions. Ninety days before the end of the fiscal year, the sponsor must file a listing of the projects covered by the group exemption, showing those that have been added or deleted since the last report was filed.[30]

APPLYING MODEL D TO THE HYPOTHETICALS

#1 — The Artists

Model D has great potential benefit to arts organizations that sponsor a large variety of projects, where each project does not have the ability to obtain its own 501(c)(3) status but is able to incorporate as a nonprofit and place its staff on a payroll.

In this hypothetical, if the Arts Consortium obtains an IRS group exemption, Amparo and Keith each can set up their own nonprofit organization following the consortium's affiliation procedures, one for the dance troupe and one for the duration of the film. Then they can apply directly to government agencies, private foundations and others for funding, in the name of their projects, using the consortium's group exemption letter. Keith could form a nonprofit corporation that would end up owning the film. Amparo, Keith and the other people who work on the projects will get the tax benefits and other advantages of being salaried employees of their own organizations.

---

[29] For example, under IRC § 509(a)(3) (a supporting organization, see Model E) or § 170(b)(1)(A)(ii) (a school).

[30] See Silverberg and Cooney, "Group Exemptions Can Save Administrative Costs for Subordinate Organizations," *Journal of Taxation of Exempt Organizations*, July/August 1993, pages 8-14, for a useful explanation of how the group exemption works.

#2 — The Human Services Project

If the hospice program is the only separate program of the church, it probably does not justify using a group exemption approach. If the hospice wanted to be a 501(c)(3) organization in its own name, it would be more straightforward, and probably easier, for the church to help the hospice to obtain its own IRS tax exemption, perhaps as a supporting organization to the church (see Model E).

#3 — The Environmental Group

Many national environmental groups do have IRS group exemptions to provide tax-exempt status to their local chapters and regional organizations. This is one of the most widespread forms of fiscal sponsorship. Often, the local chapter, rather than the national organization, will act as the fiscal sponsor for an environmental project that does not have its own exemption.

In this hypothetical, however, the FBRF is a 501(c)(4) organization, and the other intended beneficiary of funds is a foreign organization. Even if the Cordillera Club Foundation had a 501(c)(3) group exemption, neither FBRF nor the foreign group would qualify to be legally covered by it.

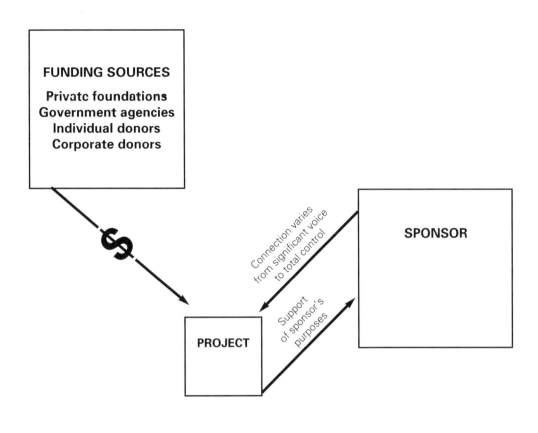

FUNDING SOURCES

Private foundations
Government agencies
Individual donors
Corporate donors

SPONSOR

Connection varies
from significant voice
to total control

Support
of sponsor's
purposes

PROJECT

MODEL E —
SUPPORTING ORGANIZATION

This model does not relieve the project of any of the details of establishing a free-standing 501(c)(3) nonprofit organization, except one. That one, however, is crucial. The project can obtain IRS classification as a public charity — which is a very valuable classification to have — without having to meet the highly technical public support test used to divide the world of 501(c)(3) organizations into private foundations, which are heavily regulated under Chapter 42 of the Internal Revenue Code, and public charities, which are free of those regulations.

If the hospice, in the human services hypothetical, gets its own 501(c)(3) status, it may avoid having to meet a public support test if it can be a "supporting organization" to the church under Model E.

An organization normally qualifies as a public charity based either on the nature of its activities (a church, school, hospital, etc.) or the broad base of its financial support (the public support test). By contrast, a Model E supporting organization (the project) does not have to concern itself with these issues. Instead, the project achieves public charity status under Section 509(a)(3) of the Internal Revenue Code by having a special relationship to a "supported organization" that does qualify, independently, as a public charity (the sponsor). The project must meet four tests under 509(a)(3):[31]

1. *The relationship test* offers three ways in which the project can be operated by, supervised by, controlled by, or connected to the sponsor. Many Model E projects will want to qualify as "operated in connection with" the sponsor, by having at least one member of the project's board of directors selected by the sponsor, who has a significant voice on the board, and by showing that the project directly engages in activities that perform the functions or carry out the purposes of the sponsor. The project should be able to demonstrate that its program is within the range of activities normally conducted by the sponsor as part of the sponsor's charitable mission.

2. *The organizational test* is met mainly by special provisions in the project's articles of incorporation, which commit the project to a supportive relationship with the sponsor.

3. *The operational test* is met by the fact that the project conducts independent programs that support the mission of the sponsor.

4. *The control test* basically requires that substantial contributors to the project (as well as their families and business enterprises) must have less than 50% of the voting power on the project's board of directors.

Model E is best suited to the project that is willing and able to obtain its own 501(c)(3) tax-exempt status, but expects to get all of its funding from

---

[31] These tests are described in greater detail in the Appendix.

fewer than five private foundations, individuals, families or business companies. Such a project would fail a public support test on its own, but by linking up with a public charity sponsor in the manner prescribed by the IRS, it can avoid classification as a private foundation. If the project has five or more unrelated private donors, or has government funding, or receives a sizable portion of its income from selling goods and services related to its exempt purposes, it can probably meet a public support test on its own.

Relationship

In Model E, the project is a legal entity totally separate from the sponsor. The links between the two organizations need be no more than the minimum required by the IRS under the relationship test of 509(a)(3). The degree of connection may vary. The project could be a subsidiary of the sponsor, with its board of directors selected entirely by the sponsor. The project and sponsor both could be controlled by a third organization. Or, in the most attenuated structure, the sponsor could have a close and continuing relationship with the project, and a significant voice in the project's policy decisions, but no power to choose any member of the project's board.

Handling of Charitable Donations

As in Model D, the Model E supporting organization can seek grants and raise funds in its own name, and the sponsor is not required to handle any funds for the project. The salient advantage of Model E is that it permits a project to seek all its funding from a single source and still qualify as a public charity due to its relationship with the sponsor. For the project that is lucky to have a wealthy patron and is willing to go through the 501(c)(3) exemption process, Model E is ideal.

Administrative Charge

No administrative charge would be imposed on the project by the sponsor, ordinarily, in a 509(a)(3) situation. However, there is nothing improper about the sponsor requiring some amount of payment from the project. The IRS recognizes that a 509(a)(3) group may support the supported organization financially as well as programmatically.

Liabilities

A sponsor has no liability at all to third parties for the acts or omissions of a project that has, as its only link with the sponsor, the minimum relationship required by 509(a)(3). However, if the project is a subsidiary of the sponsor, and the sponsor becomes involved in the day-to-day affairs and decisions of the project, a third party may reach the sponsor in a lawsuit.

Ownership

The Model E project is the sole owner of any assets that it accumulates or creates. The IRS does not require that the project's articles of incorporation state that the project's net assets shall be transferred to the sponsor upon dissolution of the project. Nevertheless, charitable trust principles under state law will demand that any successor to the assets of the project must use those assets to continue support of the sponsor as prescribed by the articles of the project. All assets received under the project's articles of incorporation during its existence are dedicated to support of the sponsor.

Tax Reporting

Section 509(a)(3) public charity status does not impose any extra tax reporting obligations upon the sponsor.[32] The project, of course, must file its own IRS Form 990 as a free-standing organization. But it is not required to supply any data to the IRS on its sources of support. There is one place on the Form 990, Schedule A, Part IV, where the project must identify the sponsor as its "supported organization."

---

[32] By contrast, a 501(c)(3) organization that applies to the IRS for classification as a public charity under a public support test must provide budget data that show it expects to receive diversified sources of support in the future. When the IRS grants this classification initially, it does so with an "advance ruling," good for five years. At the end of that period, the organization must submit its public support data, often with additional material about its fund-raising efforts, governance and activities, in order to get a permanent ruling. Many charities fail to do so, frequently out of ignorance of this special requirement, and hundreds every year are reclassified as private foundations. Even if the group gets a permanent ruling, it must continue reporting public support data every year on IRS Form 990, Schedule A, and it must monitor its sources of support carefully. Using Model E eliminates all of this.

APPLYING MODEL E TO THE HYPOTHETICALS

#1 — The Artists

Like Model D, Model E could be used by Amparo to set up her own nonprofit corporation and file returns as a tax-exempt organization. Under Model E, she would have to apply to the IRS for her organization's own 501(c)(3) tax status. If her group receives government funding in excess of one-third of its total support, it will satisfy the IRS public support test on its own. But if she doesn't receive government money, and is funded by fewer than five private sources, her best strategy might be to establish a 509(a)(3) relationship to the consortium, so that when she applies for 501(c)(3) tax status her organization won't be classified as a private foundation. The same is true for Keith and his film.

#2 — The Human Services Project

In this hypothetical, the parties involved know they want the hospice to be a separate organization. The hospice will be its own nonprofit corporation, apply for 501(c)(3) status, and file its own tax returns. Because of its special, historical relationship to the church, it is an excellent candidate for Model E. The church has public charity status by statute, and does not have to meet a public support test. The hospice should not have to meet a public support test, either. Section 509(a)(3) was designed to confer public charity status on organizations conducting programs that the sponsor would otherwise be doing itself, such as publishing houses that serve universities, or community welfare programs set up by churches. As with Hypothetical #1, Model E is a good idea if funding is provided by fewer than five private sources. But even if the hospice has many sources of income, Model E relieves the hospice of the recordkeeping and reporting burden of tracking gifts from substantial contributors and others.

#3 — The Environmental Group

Model E would not be appropriate for this hypothetical. Neither the FBRF nor the foreign organization could qualify for 501(c)(3) tax exemption, and so the further advantage of public charity status would be of no benefit.

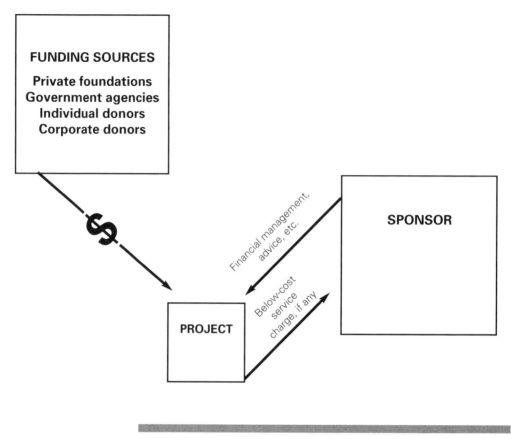

FUNDING SOURCES

Private foundations
Government agencies
Individual donors
Corporate donors

SPONSOR

Financial management,
advice, etc.

Below-cost
service
charge, if any

PROJECT

MODEL F —
TECHNICAL ASSISTANCE

In all the other models, the project relies upon the sponsor for some legal benefit or advantage under federal tax law. In Model F, the project may have complete legal independence, its own 501(c)(3) status and its own public charity classification. It has no duty to support the purposes or follow the directions of the sponsor. Instead, what the project receives from the sponsor is practical help with the details of administering a nonprofit organization that otherwise might be beyond the project's skills or capacity. Art projects like Amparo's dance troupe and Keith's film could benefit greatly from Model F, as could many other new or small organizations.

This practical help is recognized by the IRS as "technical assistance." The theory is that one nonprofit organization can fulfill its exempt purposes by providing below-cost services to aid another nonprofit to achieve its charitable work in the community. Here is a partial list of the services that could qualify as technical assistance:

- Preparation of tax-exemption applications
- Bookkeeping and accounting
- Payroll
- Preparation of tax returns
- Fund-raising
- Advertising
- Office management
- Legal services
- Insurance
- Information Technology

Notice that none of these services is charitable per se. There are for-profit businesses that provide these services in most communities. The key distinction is that technical assistance rendered by Charity A to Charity B must generally be priced below Charity A's cost of providing the service.[33] Often, the service is provided free. If the sponsor does charge the project for the service, the sponsor should be able to show that the charge is less than the sponsor's cost, including both direct expenses as well as a portion of indirect staff and overhead costs. Alternatively, the sponsor could demonstrate that the services are priced below cost because grants and donations are required to balance the

---

[33] Some of the leading IRS legal authorities on the subject of below-cost technical assistance are Rev. Rul. 69-528, 1969-2 C.B. 127 (investment services); Rev. Rul. 69-572, 1969-2 C.B. 119 (community chest office building); Rev. Rul. 71-529, 1971-2 C.B. 234 (management of endowment funds, for a nominal fee less than 15% of operating costs); Rev. Rul. 72-369, 1972-2 C.B. 245 (managerial and consulting services); *B.S.W. Group, Inc. v. Commissioner*, 70 T.C. 352 (1978) (consulting services); GCM 38447 (July 17, 1980) (insurance services); and *Airlie Foundation v. I.R.S.*, 283 F. Supp. 2d 58 (D.D.C. 2003) (conference center).

sponsor's budget by subsidizing the technical assistance services. It helps to show that the sponsor's services are priced below the market for similar services, but the sponsor will jeopardize its 501(c)(3) tax status if the sponsor's main activities consist of profitable services that are not per se charitable.[34]

Relationship

Under Model F, the relationship between sponsor and project could range from a one-time occurrence, such as help with an application for a grant or for tax-exempt status, to a full-scale management contract under which the sponsor runs the administrative operations of the project's office while the project personnel run the program. Also, Model F could be combined with the relationships established under Models B, C, D or E.

Handling of Charitable Donations

As with Models D and E, under Model F the project can seek grants and raise funds in its own name, and the sponsor is not required to handle any funds for the project. However, if the sponsor provides fund-raising, financial or office services, the sponsor's staff may physically process the project's revenues. This would be done in the name of the project, and all funds would be deposited in the project's bank account.

Administrative Charge

As discussed above, sponsors often charge for administrative services provided to projects under Model F. If the sponsor claims that providing such services to other charities for a fee is related to its exempt purposes, it should be prepared to show that the fee is established below the sponsor's actual cost, or be prepared to show some special circumstance justifying a higher charge. Unlike the other models, there is a great deal of IRS law on the proper amount that can be charged in technical assistance situations, so it is best to ask an accountant or attorney with expertise in this area for advice on setting up such a program.

---

[34] However, the sponsor could provide some services at a profit, as a secondary activity, and treat the charges as unrelated business taxable income.

Liabilities

As already noted, the sponsor and the project are completely indepen-dent and separate organizations. The liabilities between them will be governed by the contract between them, which should be in writing, and by the legal principles of agency.[35]

Ownership

The Model F project is the sole owner of any assets that it accumulates or creates.

Tax Reporting

Both the sponsor and the project have their own IRS Form 990 and other tax reporting obligations as independent organizations. If a charge is made for the technical assistance, this will be reflected on both organizations' tax returns. The sponsor will show the service charges as income related to its exempt purposes (unless it is unrelated business taxable income, in which case IRS Form 990-T must be filed). The project will show the fee paid to the spon-sor as an expense. If the sponsor is providing a variety of services, the charge may be broken down into accounting categories for bookkeeping, clerical staff, rent, telephone and other office expenses.

APPLYING MODEL F TO THE HYPOTHETICALS

#1 — The Artists

Model F alone would not meet the needs of Amparo and Keith for dance troupe and film project funding. However, if either project received a grant from the sponsor under Model C, was covered by a group exemption

---

[35] Unlike the other models, here the sponsor may actually be the agent of the project in dealings with third parties. For instance, if the sponsor is providing office staff for the project, the actions of those staff people when they deal with third parties on behalf of the project will be attributable to the project.

under Model D, or was a supporting organization under Model E, it might also benefit from the sponsor's technical assistance. This is especially true for artists, whose intense involvement with the creative process may not allow time for administration. The consortium could assist a number of art projects with legal formation, bookkeeping, clerical support, payroll, and other work necessary to maintain the projects' legal independence.

#2 — The Human Services Project

Here, technical assistance from the church is not likely to be appropriate in the long run. The church wants to be relieved of the administrative burden of running the hospice. However, during a transition period, the church may help to manage and train the personnel who eventually will operate the hospice independently.

#3 — The Environmental Group

The Model C grant relationship is probably best suited to this hypothetical. Technical assistance is not likely to be needed, because grant funds will be disbursed to FBRF and the Brazilian organization, and those groups will be able to handle their own project administration in Brazil. If technical assistance from the foundation were needed on some issue, it is important to notice that the assistance would be provided to an organization that is not a U.S. 501(c)(3) organization. This is not a problem for the sponsor, however, because if the project has qualified for a grant due to its charitable nature, it should also qualify for technical assistance.

POSTSCRIPT

CRITICISM AND COMMENTARY
1993

Even before its publication, this book began to stimulate debate and discussion about the risks and benefits of the models presented here. Two philanthropic experts who took the time to review an earlier draft manuscript of the book wrote very perceptive comments that influenced the final draft. Here are some of their remarks, in their own words.

Drummond Pike, of Tides Foundation, thought that more attention should be paid "to the necessary developmental process as a group moves from sponsored to independent status. This, in fact, is the crux of the problem, for most engaged in starting charitable projects are passionate practitioners and program experts. They are not often CPAs, management experts or administrators. As a funder or supporter of such start-ups, then, one should be most concerned about identifying the sponsorship structure which effectively trains the project founders in the rigors and realities of operating effectively in the charitable sector."

Mr. Pike was critical of Model C: "Sponsors tend to be loose in conducting supervision and requiring compliance with what rules they do have, when they are not responsible for activities of the 'preapproved grantee' and will not suffer consequences for them. Similarly, the sponsored 'grantee' will soon grow to view the sponsor as an unfortunate cost of doing business, and as having no practical impact on its daily life. The fact of the matter is that supervision and control should be an assumption underlying any system of sponsorship." He went on to say: "Clearly, Models A and B create more effective means of exercising supervision and control, for incentives exist for both sponsor and project to create a collaborative supervision relationship."

Kirke Wilson, of Rosenberg Foundation, wrote: "The term 'fiscal sponsor' is, for all the reasons you mention and others, preferable to 'fiscal agent.' In addition to placing the responsibility where it belongs, the language also, it seems to me, is likely to result in increased deliberation among sponsors about their responsibilities. Where a fiscal agent sounds like a bookkeeping function, sponsorship sounds like it entails greater supervision and liability."

Mr. Wilson felt that the hypothetical examples conveyed "the dynamism of many nonprofit enterprises in their early stages. It has seemed to me that one of the major limitations of previous discussions of fiscal agentry has been the rigidity of the categories and relationships and the failure to recognize that these young organizations are constantly growing and changing so that the tidy relationship of January may be, like children's clothes, outgrown by April. In fact, following the metaphor, nonprofit organizations may be two or more sizes at once as they move toward independence."

About Model D, Mr. Wilson remarked: "I was familiar with the group exemption but assumed that it could only be used by entities like the Catholic Church. I am impressed that you have added it to the list of ways in which a sponsorship relationship could be structured. In addition to the use of this model for large and permanent groups, it seems to me that it offers wonderful potential for clusters of small and short-term activities like those found in environmental or advocacy groups."

He concluded by saying that the presentation in this book "is positive (there are proper arrangements and not merely methods of avoiding tax laws) and grounded in what feel like real situations and problems. Because the models are so complex and require such precision, it may be useful to emphasize even more than you have the three elements of the problem:

"1. IRS rejection of conduit relationships;

"2. 501(c)(3) prohibition on private benefit;

"3. the vitality and diversity of charitable activity including the activity that is too new or too short-term to justify or allow the establishment of a free-standing 501(c)(3) organization."

Certainly, we expect that publication of this book will stimulate others to comment upon, criticize, elaborate and refine the ideas presented here. It is our hope that the definition of alternative models for fiscal sponsorship will promote the development of a common language, so that charitable organizations and their legal advisors can understand and describe more clearly the structures and relationships they have created.

LESSONS LEARNED, CONCEPTS CLARIFIED, RECENT DEVELOPMENTS

The theory and practice of fiscal sponsorship seem to be nearing a point of takeoff. From before 1993 as a barely understood method of working around the cost and complexity of separate incorporation and IRS exemption hurdles, fiscal sponsorship has come into its own, generating major foundation support, academic study, competition among sponsors for projects, spirited debate,[1] and wide recognition on the Internet. The last 15 years have been a time of experimentation with various techniques and institutionalization of the most successful.[2] In the following list of topics, we review many of the exciting manifestations of fiscal sponsorship that have emerged across America and abroad as well.

1. **Terminology**. Usage of the phrase "fiscal sponsorship" is growing rapidly.

In March 2005, a Google.com search of the term yielded 72,500 hits, as compared with 25,700 hits for "fiscal agency." The phrase "fiscal sponsor" yielded 29,100 hits; however, the term "fiscal agent" produced 244,000 hits.

The situations in which "fiscal agent" appeared were so varied and far-ranging as to defy any coherent definition. In the first 10 Google hits, only five referred to the kind of fiscal sponsorship described in this book. The other five included systems for Medicaid claims processing, financial control systems at two Illinois universities, and the Website www.investorwords.com, which

---

[1] Lee Sheppard, "Charitable Money Laundering," and Gregory Colvin, "In Defense of Fiscal Sponsorship," were published in 8 *Exempt Organization Tax Review*, 645 and 648 (Oct. 1993).

[2] An intriguing 2003 study titled "Fiscal Sponsorship: the state of a growing service" available online at www.trustforconservationinnovation.org, researched the practices of almost 20 fiscal sponsors nationwide.

defined a fiscal agent as follows: "A bank or trust company which handles fiscal matters for a corporation, including disbursement of dividend payment funds, redeeming bonds and coupons at maturity, and handling taxes related to the issuance of bonds." That obviously has nothing to do with projects sponsored by 501(c)(3) organizations. This confusing array of multiple meanings is all the more reason to avoid use of the term "fiscal agent."

Some government agencies, foundations and other funding sources persist in telling projects that don't have their own 501(c)(3) exemption to find a "fiscal agent." The March 2005 Google search showed that the National Endowment for the Arts used the term in its sample online agreement for art projects to be sponsored by an eligible 501(c)(3) grantee. The Endowment for Health, a New Hampshire foundation, did the same.

In the charitable world, one does occasionally see the rare case of a true "fiscal agent" (also known as a "custodial fund," see paragraph 5 below), a transparent financial relationship where one party receives, holds and expends funds that legally belong to another. Aside from that circumstance, the term fiscal agency is absolutely not equivalent to or interchangeable with fiscal sponsorship. This misleading and legally improper usage ought to be corrected at every opportunity. Those who are conversant in the proper terminology should be vigilant in calling upon those who draft application forms, instructions and other documents to stop using "fiscal agent."[3]

Granted, calling a fiscal sponsor a "fiscal agent" is probably a benign bit of linguistic slippage in most situations. However, if the correct terms and legal concepts are not understood and used at the outset of a fiscal sponsor relationship, it is very possible that the parties will find out much later, in an IRS audit or in a lawsuit, that they did not structure the relationship in a manner that protects the rights and duties of the funding source, the sponsor and the project.

Quite a few terms have emerged in the lexicon of fiscal sponsorship. Some fit well into best practices, others seem to give the wrong signals.

---

[3] Thanks to the Council on Foundations and author Jane Nober for the article entitled "Fiscal Agency Versus Fiscal Sponsorship," in *Foundation News & Commentary*, November/December 2004, for reinforcing this argument.

Examples are:

Inaccurate/Confusing/Improper	Relatively Safe
Fiscal agency	Fiscal sponsorship
Fiscal agent	Fiscal sponsor
Earmarked for the X project	In support of the purposes of the X project
Acting as a conduit	Exercising discretion and control
Pass-through	Regrant
Funnel	Platform
Intermediary	Umbrella
Partnership, joint venture	Collaborative
Cooperative	Consortium, coalition
Shell	Cluster
Autonomous	Accountable
Laundering	Incubation
Go-between	Steward

Readers may benefit from knowing that two of these terms, "fiscal agent" and "conduit," have had a mixed reception recently in federal courts and federal tax interpretations.

a. Fiscal agent

In the case of *Briggs* v. *Chesapeake Volunteers in Youth Services*, 68 F.Supp. 2d 711 (E.D. Va. 1999), an employee of a nonprofit corporation sued to collect more than 1,000 hours of overtime pay under the Fair Labor Standards Act. The plaintiff claimed that his nonprofit employer, Chesapeake Volunteers, was actually a "public agency" subject to the fair labor act because, among other reasons, his paychecks were cut by the City of Chesapeake. The court dismissed the claim, disregarding "the artificial connection of the City acting as the fiscal agent for the CVYS" and noting that "the City does not claim any oversight over the CVYS…." In other words, the court saw the fiscal agency as a meaningless arrangement where the City was handling the payroll but had no discretion or control over the nonprofit organization or its employees.

Again, in *Salm* v. *Broncato, et al.*, 149 F.Supp. 2d (C.D. Ill. 2001), the plaintiff sued in federal court claiming to be an employee of the State of

Illinois. She alleged that her contract with the Illinois Transition Consortium was not renewed, in violation of her civil rights, but it appears the Consortium was not a legal entity, just a federal grant program to assist the developmentally disabled. One of the three state agencies in the Consortium executed an employment agreement with her and disbursed her paychecks, but only as a "fiscal agent" for the Consortium, the result being that the State of Illinois was never really her employer; it was just passing on the money, so the State was not responsible and she lost the case.

In another case, *Esperanza Peace and Justice Center* v. *City of San Antonio*, 316 F.Supp. 2d (W.D. Tex. 2001), the City Council voted to discontinue Esperanza's arts funding. Esperanza brought a "viewpoint discrimination" suit in federal court, saying that the funding was cut because it supported gay and lesbian issues. Not only did Esperanza win the case for damages, but so did two unincorporated associations, Media Project and VAN, for which Esperanza served as "sponsor and fiscal agent" (perhaps not sure which was the correct term, the court used both).

The IRS has issued several private letter rulings using "fiscal agent" in connection with the administration of government or private funds used to support tax-exempt organizations, but with no consistent definition of that term.[4] The bottom line: the term "fiscal agent" is unreliable.

b. Conduit

The IRS continues to take a dim view of "conduit" organizations, especially those used to make payments to charitable organizations for the benefit of specific individuals named by the donors. In a lengthy 1996 article titled "Conduit Organizations – Charitable Deductibility and Exemption Issues," IRS attorneys Ruth Rivera Huetter and Bill Brockner link their discussion of conduit problems to a critique of "fiscal agents" that "launder" donations, such as tuition payments for the donor's children to attend private school.[5] They ana-

---

[4] Private Letter Rulings 9611044, 200106041, and 200426010.

[5] FY1996 Exempt Organizations Continuing Professional Education textbook found at www.irs.gov, under "Charities & Nonprofits," listed as "EO Tax Law Training." The IRS works to combat conduit arrangements in many areas of federal tax law. Another example is IRC Section 7701(l), and the issuance of "conduit financing" regulations by the IRS in August 1995, addressing methods used by foreign taxpayers using intermediate entities to obtain the benefit of U.S. tax treaties. Treas. Reg. 1.881-3 et seq.

lyze the notorious case of the Owl Foundation, which had operated as a 501(c)(3) charity for many years, soliciting donors to make tax-deductible contributions to be used to pay for their children's school tuition, plus a 15% administrative fee. The IRS revoked the foundation's tax exemption back to the date it was formed in 1977, denied tax deductions to donors named Mr. and Mrs. Graves, and sought tax penalties against them for fraud and negligence. The U.S. Tax Court upheld the denial of deductions and negligence penalties.[6]

In another fascinating ruling, the IRS considered a religious organization that solicited contributions to cover tuition costs of seminary students. Parents and relatives could name the student they wanted to support, but the organization cautioned the donor not to put the student's name on the check, rather "on the envelope or a separate paper." The organization made several statements in its literature and policy manual that the disposition of all contributions "rests with the board of directors," but that it "honors the donor's designation whenever possible" and "takes donor's designations into account as a matter of accountability and integrity." The IRS stated that a gift is not a deductible contribution "if the facts show that the charity is merely a conduit to a particular person." It found that the organization "refutes its own statement of control by going on to say" that donor designations are "a matter of accountability."[7] Two possible lessons here: (1) everything else about a fiscal sponsorship can be fine, but the entire structure can be undermined by a few ill-chosen words, and (2) no magic words about discretion and control can completely insulate a fiscal sponsorship from attack; the IRS can still find that a conduit arrangement exists by examining all the "facts and circumstances."

Different facts were presented in *Hubert* v. *Commissioner*, T.C.M. 1993-482, where a Baptist church asked a church member (not a relative) to sponsor two missionaries from the church, one working in Peru and one in overseas radio. The member did so for many years, then died leaving $100,000 in each of two trusts to support the missionaries during their lives, through retirement. The estate claimed charitable deductions that were denied by the IRS but the Tax Court disagreed. Citing the *Davis* Mormon missionary case

---

[6] *Graves v. Commissioner*, T.C.M. 1994-616.

[7] Technical Advice Memorandum 9405003.

(Model X), the court found that the trust payments went to two charitable mission organizations, not to the missionaries personally, and that the charities possessed sufficient discretion and control to allow the contributions to be deductible. Finding that the charities had discretion over the "amounts of funds to be used and the methods of using those funds" (including construction of foreign medical clinics), the court determined that the trusts were not "a mere conduit to funnel money to an individual" but were to benefit the general public.

Sometimes, donors to college scholarship funds try to express a preference for relatives or persons with the same surname. In a 1995 ruling, the IRS permitted a charitable estate tax deduction for a university scholarship fund containing a requirement that at least once every 15 years, a scholarship would go to a student (if one applied) with one of four surnames (not necessarily related to grantor). Otherwise, scholarships could be awarded to any student in the university's discretion. The IRS ruled that "the class of beneficiaries was not so small and identifiable as to defeat the charitable deduction."[8]

2. **Relative Popularity of the Models.** By far, Model A (direct project) is the most popular, followed by Model C (preapproved grant relationship). More about those models later.

Pure Model B (independent contractor project), where the sponsor contracts out the entire project to a single contractor, is not as common as one might imagine. We find, though, that many Model A direct projects make some use of consultants and other independent contractors to do their work. Recently, the IRS approved what appeared to be a Model B arrangement whereby a 501(c)(3) charity commissioned a musical work by a specific composer, supported by a tax-deductible donation from a married couple who expressed a desire to support the composer's work, but the charity retained unrestricted control and discretion over the funds.[9]

Model D (group exemption) has not become a popular fiscal sponsorship vehicle, despite its potential, and continues to be most typical of parent-affiliate groups organized geographically. For instance, Toastmasters International, a parent organization located in Orange County, California, has char-

---

[8] Private Letter Ruling 9527026.

tered more than 10,000 Toastmasters Clubs in the United States and abroad, conferring 501(c)(3) status on the clubs by way of the group exemption.

Model E (supporting organization) is a popular vehicle for donors seeking an alternative to a private foundation, but from an operational standpoint, it may be less common for projects to incorporate and obtain tax status as supporting organizations to their sponsors. Some variations of Model E, especially the "Type 3" form, where the relationship between supporting and supported organizations is most attenuated, have drawn criticism in the media, in Congress, and among IRS officials.[10]

Model F (technical assistance) is a very common phenomenon, but due to the low profile of the service provided, it is hard to measure. The most prominent examples probably are community foundations that offer financial administration to charities in their regions. For instance, the Greater Kansas City Community Foundation's Client Accounting Services has more than 60 local and national clients.[11]

Model X (payments "for the use of" sponsor) was a theoretically intriguing trust arrangement that emerged from litigation over the funding of Mormon missionaries, but we have not seen it imitated outside of that context.

Reminder to readers: If the project does not have its own 501(c)(3)

---

[9] Private Letter Ruling 200250029. In another case, *Greene v. Commissioner*, T.C.M. 1996-531, a minister of the Assemblies of God church was a missionary in Bangladesh. He set his own work days and hours, chose the type of work to perform, did not communicate with the church very often, and was not directly supervised by the church. The Tax Court ruled that Mr. Greene was an independent contractor rather than an employee, given the lack of control the church had over him. He personally raised donations to the church to support his mission for four years. However, the court did not address the question whether the church still retained enough discretion and control to allow the donations to be tax-deductible.

[10] For a good discussion, see "Public Charity Status on the Razor's Edge," by Ron Shoemaker and Bill Brockner, in the FY1997 Exempt Organizations Continuing Professional Education textbook found at www.irs.gov, under "Charities & Nonprofits," listed as "EO Tax Law Training." Also, see "Final Report of the Panel on the Nonprofit Sector," (June 2005) page 45, by Independent Sector, available on its Website.

[11] Nonprofits providing management services to charities may not qualify for charitable tax exemption themselves. In *Sacred Heart Healthcare System v. Pennsylvania*, 673 A.2d 1021 (Pa. Cmwlth. Ct. 1996), a state court found that a nonprofit organization created by a hospital did not qualify for sales tax exemption because the accounting, human resource, administration and data processing services it provided for a fee to the hospital did not have a charitable purpose.

---

status, it must find a Model A, B or C fiscal sponsor to receive deductible donations and most grants. Model D, E, F and X sponsors provide other benefits to projects, but do not legally receive funds for them.

3. **Model A Direct Project.** This model is very popular because the project has none of the responsibilities of maintaining separate legal existence. The project has no board of directors, no tax return, and usually has no bank account of its own, except perhaps petty cash. The sponsor handles all financial administration for the project, from payroll to health plan to tax filings to insurance, and can achieve great efficiencies by issuing checks from one bank account for dozens of projects, posted to separate accounts for each of them. The project just needs to submit timely check requests and be sure it raises enough revenue to keep its project account in the black.

The main challenge of Model A is, of course, the complete liability borne by the sponsor for everything the project does. Managing such liabilities requires attention to insurance coverage and risk management, as discussed in paragraph g. on page 73.

For those who have fiscal sponsorship arrangements, but are unsure which model they are using, the first question to ask is: "Are the people running the project organized as a separate legal entity?" If they are not, the arrangement is most likely Model A.

A number of fascinating issues have arisen in connection with Model A projects, as follows:

a. **Advisory Committee.** Some Model A sponsors require that a project have an advisory committee overseeing its work. This promotes a collective sense of responsibility for the project, and serves as a means of holding the project director accountable. By requiring an advisory committee, the sponsor can screen out projects that are little more than a personal enterprise of the project director. Typically, such committees include funders, professional colleagues, community members and senior project staff. They serve as a sounding board for the project director's plans, ideas and problems, and often have authority delegated to them by the sponsor's board of directors to supervise the operation of the project. The advisory committee should not be called a "board of directors," because that suggests the project is its own legal entity and that the board has independent power to control the affairs of the project.

b. **Unincorporated Association**. It is often advisable to form the project's advisory committee as an unincorporated association. This involves little more than signing a form of bylaws called "articles of association" to govern the committee's decision-making process. The committee may then file a simple notice with the secretary of state in the state where the project is located. Thus acquiring the capacity to "sue and be sued," the advisory committee has the legal power to enter into a fiscal sponsorship agreement with the sponsor,[12] and it thereby acquires the right to enforce its side of the agreement as a contract in court. This could be critical at the time the project decides to "leave the nest" of the sponsor. If the advisory committee has the right to terminate the sponsorship and transfer all assets and liabilities associated with the project to another sponsor (assuming funders do not object), the project has real "portability."

c. **Transfers of Projects, In and Out**. Sometimes, a Model A project comes into being with one sponsor and stays with it until its work is done, its funding runs out, or its people give up and move on. More often, projects transfer from one 501(c)(3) sponsor to another, and this may occur once, twice, or many times. When a new project applies to a 501(c)(3) organization for sponsorship, it may turn out that the project had a former sponsor, in which case the two sponsors must sign an agreement transferring the project assets and liabilities from the old one to the new one. Because the advisory committee will also be a party to the new sponsorship, these become three-party agreements. A similar transfer agreement is required when the project moves on, including in the circumstance where the project has incorporated and obtained IRS recognition of its 501(c)(3) status. In this "exit" situation, a transfer agreement is needed to move the project assets and liabilities from the sponsor to the project's own new corporation.

d. **Common Uses**. Some of the popular uses of Model A sponsorships are:

1) **Incubation**. In the early stages of its life cycle, a project develops its programs under the wing of a fiscal sponsor that handles all financial administration; the project determines whether it is likely to succeed, then spins off

---

[12]Readers are cautioned that the Fiscal Sponsorship Grant Agreement in the Appendix is designed for Model C, not Model A, situations. Visit www.silklaw.com for Model A sample agreements and for transfer and exit agreements discussed in the next paragraph.

into its own 501(c)(3) nonprofit corporation when it is financially viable. These can range from small mental health projects to multimillion-dollar civic facility construction projects. Community Partners, located in Los Angeles, a 501(c)(3) fiscal sponsor spun off by the California Community Foundation, specializes in incubation of new charities.

2) **Clusters of Similar Projects.** Some projects would never be large enough to succeed on their own, but by sharing financial administration, as well as legal and tax status, with similar educational programs, environmental projects, artistic endeavors, public health research projects, or policy initiatives, they can thrive. Projects supported by government programs such as Head Start, AmeriCorps and Community Development Block Grants, may be grouped together in a single regional or local organization. Public Health Institute, Marin Community Action, Earth Island Institute and Bay Area Community Resources are four examples of clustering.

3) **Short-Term Projects.** Model A is perfect for events such as conferences and programs that just need a collection point to receive and spend funds for temporary employees, contractors and vendors, rather than a new, separate legal organization. When the mayor of San Francisco needed a fiscal sponsor for his Small Business Forum, or to host the annual convention of mayors of U.S. cities, he turned to CIF of The San Francisco Foundation for the receipt and expenditure of private funds.

4) **Sudden Needs.** A disaster or other immediate need for charitable work in a community often results in creation of a Model A project because there is simply no time to go through the legal and tax formalities of organizing a new entity. For example, when 12-year-old Polly Klaas was kidnapped in Petaluma, California, in 1993, a fund was established within the local Petaluma Junior High School PTA to support the search effort. Several weeks later, when the IRS recognized the Polly Klaas Foundation as tax-exempt, the assets and liabilities of the search fund were transferred from the PTA to the new foundation.

5) **Joint Funding Collaboratives.** Often, a consortium of private and community foundations will come together in a state or region to accomplish joint work in public education, preschool, criminal justice, neighborhood rehabilitation or other priority areas. One of the community foundations, or a stand-alone fiscal sponsor, may act as the Model A sponsor for the collabora-

tive, aggregating all the foundations' grants, paying the staff and vendors, and reporting the project on its tax return. For example, CIF of The San Francisco Foundation sponsors the Foundation Consortium for School-Linked Services, a project based in Sacramento and funded by a group of public and private foundations interested in the delivery of community services through public school sites.

6) **Coalitions.** A coalition of operating charities may gather together to pursue a common goal, such as lobbying for funding for breast cancer treatment for low-income women or for school reform or to expand wilderness areas in a specific state or national forest. Like the joint funding collaborative, one of the members of the coalition may act as a Model A sponsor of the effort, handling all receipts and disbursements.

7) **Platforms for Social Change.** The Tides Center, a fiscal sponsor organization spun off by the Tides Foundation in San Francisco, is well known for launching new progressive social change projects. Conservatives use fiscal sponsors to promote emergent ideological movements, too. Prior to the Republican capture of a majority in the U.S. House of Representatives in 1994, Speaker Newt Gingrich promoted a cable television program called "Renewing American Civilization," which had two fiscal sponsors (Abraham Lincoln Opportunity Foundation and Kennesaw State College) before coming to rest in a new 501(c)(3) entity named Progress and Freedom Foundation. Gingrich needed charitable sponsorship to raise tax-deductible funds for this college extension course, which was strategically aimed to provide an educational foundation for the Republican political cause.[13]

e. **Staying Solvent.** Without strict financial discipline, projects running a deficit can bring down a Model A sponsor, depleting the sponsor's general funds and invading funds held for other projects. Some Model A sponsors do not allow a project to continue without a balance to cover at least a month of payroll and expenses, and do not allow external or internal borrowing. The sponsor has full liability for each project, so it must be ready to lay off employ-

---

[13]Gregory Colvin, "Learning the Lessons of the Gingrich Affair," 11 *Journal of Taxation of Exempt Organizations 82,* (Sept./Oct. 1999). The House Ethics Committee censured and fined Speaker Gingrich in the course of examining his use of the fiscal sponsors, but the IRS eventually cleared the sponsors after its own charitable tax law investigation.

---

ees, notify vendors, and terminate a project if funding is in doubt.

Probably the most notorious collapse of a fiscal sponsor occurred in 1997 when a major sponsor of documentary films, Media Network, suddenly ceased operations, citing "a rapidly increasing deficit." Because its liabilities exceeded the assets in its various accounts, it could only offer the filmmakers 80% of what they expected, and many received much less. According to the New York Times, "Media Network had long had a practice of occasionally tapping the filmmakers' money in hard times, paying the money back when the corporation was flush."[14] A lawsuit and attorney general investigation came next, focused on the charitable trust doctrine requiring funds to be used for the purposes specified by donors.

f. **Employees**. Realizing that all of the project employees are employees of the Model A sponsor, it must be understood that they all come under the same personnel policies, same health plan or plans, same retirement options, and other benefits and rules. Projects cannot depart from these standards without potentially causing the Model A sponsor to violate nondiscrimination rules and other labor laws. The sponsor's board of directors is ultimately responsible for the supervision of all project employees, even though authority to hire, fire and supervise employees on a daily basis may be delegated to project directors and/or advisory committees. When a project transfers from one sponsor to another, this is often done with a clean cutoff of employment and no assurance of employment by the new sponsor. Accrued leave must be paid to the employee by the old sponsor or assumed by the new sponsor to the extent it hires the same employees.

Some or all of the project personnel may be volunteers rather than employees. With them the sponsor should be careful about promising jobs or retroactive pay if funding becomes available, and may need legal help with harassment policies, photo releases, and other legal disclosures volunteers should sign.

g. **Insurance**. Model A fiscal sponsors must become expert in insurance matters. One large community fiscal sponsor has a motto of buying insurance

---

[14] Janny Scott, "Filmmakers' Off-Screen Drama," *New York Times*, March 25, 1998, page B3. It is not clear whether Media Network funded the films as Model A direct projects or Model C regrants.

"by the truckload." With such disparate endeavors under one roof, insurers may raise questions about (and decline to cover) certain types of activity; e.g., events where alcoholic beverages are provided, programs involving care of children, adoption services, operation of vehicles and machinery, and sports or outdoor activities. Model A sponsors go back and forth with projects and insurance companies over exclusions, special policies and limits, additional insureds, etc., often passing on any added premiums to the projects responsible for exposure to risks. Insurance of all kinds, especially general liability and medical, can be acquired quicker and at less cost by the project through its sponsor's carriers than would be possible on its own.

h. **Donations.** As the 1993 edition states, it is preferable for donation checks to be made payable to the sponsor's legal name. This is the best way for the donor to be sure that the gift is made to a recognized 501(c)(3) that can receive deductible donations. In the memo line of the check, or in accompanying documentation, the project's name can be indicated. However, we are aware that checks are often made payable to the Model A project's name, which the sponsor then deposits to a bank account in the sponsor's name. While this is not an ideal practice, it can be done legitimately. After all, the Model A project has no separate legal existence, and its name is really a "trade name" or "DBA" (doing business as) that belongs to the sponsor. To remove any doubt that the donation has gone to a proper tax-exempt entity, the paperwork used to solicit the gift, and/or to acknowledge it after it is given, should clearly state that "X project is a program of Y sponsor, a 501(c)(3) public charity" so that the donor has a document showing the legal name of the organization to which he or she has contributed.

i. **Leaving the Nest.** This phenomenon has now been the object of serious academic study. Wendy Strickland wrote a master's thesis for the graduate program in nonprofit administration at the University of San Francisco in 2001, titled "Leaving the Nest: Why Fiscally-sponsored Projects Seek Independence." Her research identified six important factors: an economic equation that favored independent provision of essential services; the presence of a previously established plan to separate; a desire to brand the project's name separate from the fiscal sponsor's; a wish to avoid redundant administrative systems; the actual presence of redundant administrative systems; and a sense that leaving the sponsor was a natural part of the project's maturation.

4. **Model C Preapproved Grant Relationship**. For some fiscal sponsors, such as 501(c)(3) funds attached to 501(c)(4) advocacy groups, Model C is the only arrangement made, because the sponsors do not operate any programs directly. The sponsor may have a primary relationship with a single grantee, with highly evolved systems of joint fundraising, and sponsor supervision and control over grants made to the 501(c)(4) project. The Sierra Club Foundation and the Sierra Club have such an arrangement. Other sponsors use Model C as a better alternative than Model A for projects with inherently risky activities. The project needs to be able to manage its own financial affairs, maintain its own payroll, carry appropriate levels of insurance, and file its own tax returns. In addition, the project is required to identify one or more specific charitable activities eligible for grants from the sponsor, and file timely reports on its progress toward achieving the sponsor's charitable purposes.

Some of the interesting issues that can arise with Model C projects are:

a. **Array of Projects**. A broader range of projects can benefit from Model C fiscal sponsorship than Model A. They may include individual authors, artists, musicians, documentary filmmakers,[15] or Web-based enthusiasts. They may be located in the United States or abroad.[16] They may be sole proprietors, partnerships, for-profit corporations, or nonprofit social welfare groups, trade unions, business associations, or social clubs, so long as they are conducting specific charitable projects.

b. **Accounting, Discretion and Control**. In addition to the IRS require-

---

[15] Since Ken Burns' "The Civil War" and the expansion of cable TV, a lively marketplace for sponsorship of documentaries has developed, from Film Arts Foundation and Bay Area Video Coalition, to International Documentary Association in Los Angeles, to a number of regional sponsors and public television stations. See Michael P. Lucas, "Now on PBS, Courtesy of the Tax Man," *Los Angeles Times*, Oct. 27, 1997.

[16] Stephen Greene, "'Friends' of Foreign Charities Help Donors Get Tax Breaks on Gifts," *Chronicle of Philanthropy*, June 13, 1996. International fiscal sponsorship includes American charities linked to a single foreign institution, using the pattern the IRS approved in Rev. Rul. 66-79, as well as U.S. charities embracing an entire continent or field of work, e.g. Give2Asia, CAFAmerica, Open Society Institute, and WILD Foundation. After the Sept. 11, 2001, terrorist attacks, fiscal sponsors making overseas grants have had to increase their level of due diligence when screening grantees.

ment that the sponsor maintain "discretion and control" over funds received and granted to Model C projects, GAAP (generally accepted accounting principles) may call for additional steps to be taken to establish clearly that the sponsor is not simply acting as an intermediary for a transfer of assets to a specific ultimate recipient. The sponsor must retain "variance power" over funds earmarked to support the purposes of the project. The best practice is for the Model C sponsor to inform donors in writing along the following lines:

> For legal and accounting purposes, we need to notify you of our "variance power" over funds donated to us in support of this program. Under our fiscal sponsorship agreement with ABC project, we retain full discretion and control over the use of such funds to accomplish the charitable purposes of the approved program. This power includes the unilateral right to redirect funds to a different beneficiary who can accomplish the purposes of this program if for some reason ABC cannot. (See Interpretation No. 42 of the Financial Accounting Standards Board's Statement No. 116.)

The span of the sponsor's discretion and control may vary in practice. There is some language in IRS precedents, such as Revenue Ruling 66-79 in the Appendix, indicating that the Model C sponsor has "the right to withdraw approval of the grant and use the funds for other charitable, scientific or educational purpose." One cannot tell from the ruling whether such absolute discretion to use the funds for a completely different purpose — in another country, for public health instead of the arts, or to send kids to camp instead of producing a film — was key to the IRS approval in that ruling. We have seen Model C relationships that do give the sponsor that much latitude. More commonly, however, the sponsor's range of options is somewhat limited by the terms and conditions of the donors' gifts (and, consequently, by the common law of charitable trusts), to certain purposes, to use in a particular location, or to the production of a certain charitable outcome. We believe that the essential right that the Model C sponsor must have is the freedom to select, and if necessary replace, the person or entity who will receive the grant funds. The Model C sponsor can legally bind itself to spend the funds only for a specific charitable purpose, but it cannot agree to dedicate funds to a purpose that can only be achieved by one specific grantee.

As with Model A, the Model C sponsor must keep each project fund in the black, and not support one project by dipping into funds set aside for another project.[17]

c. **Incubation**. Model C can provide a good way to incubate a new non-profit charitable organization. For the first few months while the new entity is awaiting IRS recognition of its exemption, the sponsor can receive grants and donations, provide charitable gift acknowledgements and receipts to donors, and regrant funds to the new corporation so it can commence operations immediately. However, some new 501(c)(3) entities actually prefer Model A fiscal sponsorship while they are waiting for their IRS letter, so they can postpone having to manage their own bank account, payroll and vendor bills until the letter comes.

5. **Other Models: True Fiscal Agents.** Occasionally, true "fiscal agency" arrangements are created. Suppose five charities co-sponsor a fund-raising event, and one agrees to collect the revenue, deposit it in its bank account, and split it five ways afterward. The donor gets a receipt showing the names of all five charities. While the lead charity temporarily possessed all the funds, it never legally owned more than one-fifth of the revenue, and would only report the one-fifth on its Form 990 tax return. These arrangements are also called "custodial funds" or "common paymasters," where the lead charity is truly acting as an agent for itself and the others. A written agreement signed by all participating charities is a good way to document the process for handling funds and establish their ownership shares.

6. **Intellectual Property**. Increasingly, intellectual property matters are important in all types of fiscal sponsorships and they are frequently overlooked.

Sponsors and projects are most aware of the cash fund balance maintained by the sponsor for the project, and are usually aware of unpaid bills and other known liabilities associated with the project. They are often much less conscious of intangible assets such as trademarks, copyrights,[18] licenses, mail-

---

[17] See paragraph 3.e. Staying Solvent, above.

[18] William Hutton and Cynthia Rowland, "The Inurement Rule and Ownership of Copyrights," 9 *Exempt Organization Tax Review*, 813 (April 1994).

---

ing lists, and valuable assets created with computers and disseminated via Internet Websites. Sponsors and projects need to be deliberate in handling the identification, enumeration, ownership, usage and transfer of such assets.

Often, the inquiry can begin with the question, "Who created this?" Depending on whether a name or logo, an article or a software program, a mural or photograph was created by project employees, independent contractors, volunteers, outsiders — or perhaps the project's founder, but long before the sponsorship commenced — the intellectual property issues can be complicated and solutions elusive. The sponsor may need to wrestle with questions such as: Did the project create or acquire this work or did it infringe someone's copyright? Is this a "work made for hire"? Did the independent contractor assign all rights to the work product to the sponsor? Do we have an oral license that should be put in writing? How can we compile a full inventory of this project's intellectual property so that it can be transferred, along with its tangible assets and liabilities, to another sponsor or to the project's new 501(c)(3) entity?

These questions are most acute with Model A projects. Model C project agreements can provide for the project to retain all tangible or intangible property it obtains or creates. A Model A sponsor needs experienced intellectual-property legal counsel to help identify, inventory, protect and convey intangible assets. They may be more valuable than the project's cash balance.

7. **Other Resources and Benefits.** Many sponsors offer much more than 501(c)(3) tax deductibility to their projects. Some offer office space, furniture and equipment, computer systems, fingerprinting, insurance coverage, and help with organizational development. Model A sponsors can provide access to a nonprofit postal permit, sales tax and other exemptions, personnel benefits and human resource management, and the benefit of the sponsor's compliance with state audit requirements, local open meeting rules, and charitable solicitation laws. A sponsor can get creative with its IRS lobbying allowance under Section 501(h) or under the "insubstantial part" test, assigning more than 5% or 20% of annual project expenses to certain projects that need to lobby, because other projects will spend nothing on lobbying.[19]

---

[19] However, donations earmarked for lobbying purposes are not tax-deductible. Rev. Rul. 80-275, 1980-2 C.B. 69.

---

8. **Sponsorship Policies.** In addition to the basic fiscal sponsorship agreement, sponsors should develop a set of "sponsorship policies" to govern expectations that sponsor and project should have of each other, such as:

- Requirements to apply for sponsorship
- Composition and operation of advisory committee
- Review, approval and transmission of fund-raising materials
- Handling of donations and earned income
- Fees and additional charges
- Signature authority
- Accounts payable
- Procedures for payroll and check requests
- Periodic reports of income, expense and fund balance, provided by sponsor to project
- Periodic reports of operations and accomplishments, provided by project to sponsor
- Requirements for fund balance to cover X days of payroll and costs
- Responsibility for drafting and submitting grant reports to funding sources
- Detailed personnel policies
- The project's external use of the sponsor's name; use of other sponsors
- Code of ethics, conflict of interest policy

Sponsors should pay attention to the professional level of project directors, especially if a specialized form of business is involved. For instance, if a project director who is mainly a fund-raiser is in charge of preliminary work on a civic construction project, the process of engaging architects and environmental consultants may require the skills of a professional construction manager at a very early stage. Likewise, it is easy for directors of new projects they have never done before to get in over their heads—making films, producing events, running a lobbying campaign—so sponsors must call in an expert before the project becomes overextended with contractual obligations.

9. **Pledges.** Because contributions to fiscal sponsors are almost always dedicated to specific purposes, it is important to plan what to do if the project purpose cannot be accomplished. Sometimes, funding sources want unspent funds returned or specify other options in grant agreements. Other times,

where the sponsor seeks pledges from individuals to support a project, a standard form pledge agreement states when the pledge will and will not be enforced, and gives the donor options in the event the sponsorship is transferred or the project is modified or abandoned. Alternatives may include a pro rata refund to donors or conveyance of the donation to another, similar project, especially if the donor has already taken a tax deduction. If the sponsor would be reluctant to enforce a pledge of an unwilling donor, words like "pledge" and "commit" should not be used. It is better to use a phrase like "intention to give" that does not imply a legal obligation.

Recently, American charities have been challenged to honor the specific intent of donors reacting to the September 11 terrorist attacks and the December 2004 Indian Ocean tsunami. Old policies under which the charity permitted itself to use any donation for general support, disregarding the donor's wish to direct his or her gift to relief of a particular disaster, have had to fall in the face of public pressure. Most charities responding to modern disasters (really acting as fiscal sponsors setting up Model A direct project funds on short notice) take careful steps, such as defining the scope of the fund, communicating that scope to potential donors, asking for donor consent to change the scope, and even closing solicitations when donations can no longer be used effectively.

10. **Fund-Raising Help.** To comply with tax rules, sponsors are responsible to give proper written receipts to contributors, and keep cumulative records of gifts and grants from the same sources over four-year public support periods. Sponsors can also set up brokerage accounts to receive and liquidate donations of securities, and can even take automobiles, equipment and other forms of property.

When incubating new 501(c)(3) organizations with Model C regrants, all payments from the fiscal sponsor to the project count as public support, although the original funding source may have been private.

The name of the sponsor, if it reflects the goodwill of a community foundation or other prestigious charity, helps encourage donors to give.

Some fiscal sponsors have struck upon a novel way to assist in fund raising for their projects by listing them on the sponsor's Website, showcasing the project's goals and activities, with a mechanism for donors to make credit card contributions in support of the purposes of each project. For examples, see CIF of The San Francisco Foundation at www.tsffcif.org, Film Arts Foundation at www.filmarts.org, and Fractured Atlas at www.fracturedatlas.org.

11. **Administrative Fees**. Anecdotal evidence indicates a very wide range of fees charged for fiscal sponsorship, and a fair degree of price competition in some areas. There are sponsors who charge nothing to take on a project, and there are universities that reputedly charge 40 percent of the total budget for grant-funded public health research projects. Even the interest that may accrue on funds held by a sponsor for a project can be the subject of bargaining; some sponsors keep all the interest, some allocate all of it to the project, and some split the interest between them. In truth, it is the sponsor's money. The amount of interest that, say, a $100,000 project can generate from the few thousand it keeps in a bank account for a few months each year may be negligible.

12. **IRS Recognition**. Despite the fact that fiscal sponsorship is not a term defined by federal tax statutes or regulations, IRS officials have made helpful comments about it. Shortly after publication of the first edition, in an internal training article entitled "Community Foundations," IRS attorneys George Johnson and David Jones found "nothing inherently wrong with fiscal sponsorship. ... However, it can and has been misused." They go on to present hypothetical illustrations of legitimate fiscal sponsorship arrangements (consistent with models described in this book), contrasted with improper conduit arrangements.[20]

There are many more topics, large and small, in the field of fiscal sponsorship worth extended discussion. Fortunately, these printed pages do not need to cover all of them. With the advent of the Internet, readers can have access to Websites where interesting nuances and sudden changes can be presented and explored. We plan to maintain two sites. At www.fiscalsponsorship.com, we expect to post new developments since the latest edition of this book. Within our law firm's Website at www.silklaw.com, we will post exemplars of sponsorship agreements and other useful documents.

We are especially intrigued by the possibility that the San Francisco

---

[20]FY1994 Exempt Organizations Continuing Professional Education textbook, accessible at www.irs.gov, under "Charities & Nonprofits," listed as "EO Tax Law Training."

Study Center's impending publication of a directory of fiscal sponsors will lead to a coalescing of similar groups interested in sharing information about problems and best practices in fiscal sponsorship. Some natural affiliations may develop among fiscal sponsors in the arts, environment, public health, documentary film, community foundations, and international funding. We may soon see regional or national conferences of fiscal sponsors, and virtual meetings using online facilities. All of this will be welcome.

We also hope for continuing efforts to elevate the legal and ethical standards of conduct among fiscal sponsors and projects, and the quick identification and elimination of disreputable practices. As we have seen in other parts of the charitable world, when bad practices emerge unchecked, the pattern of exposure in the mass media, litigation and legislative remedy often distorts and complicates the beneficial work done by public-spirited leaders. In this realm, foundations and other funding sources are well-positioned to support high standards by insisting on real compliance with the legal requirements of fiscal sponsorship, rather than making expedient use of a "fiscal agent's" 501(c)(3) exempt status to issue a grant.

We are pleased at the positive reaction that the initial publication of this book received in the charitable sector, and with this new edition we look forward to participating in constructive dialogue about the future benefits to our society that can flow from the right use of fiscal sponsorship.

APPENDIX

FISCAL SPONSORSHIP GRANT AGREEMENT FOR MODEL C*

On _____, 20__, _____ (Grantor) decided that financial support of the project described in the cover letter accompanying this Agreement will further Grantor's tax-exempt purposes. Therefore, Grantor has created a restricted fund designated for such project, and has decided to grant all amounts that it may deposit to that fund, less any administrative charge as set forth below, to _____ (Grantee), subject to the following terms and conditions:

1. Grantee shall provide Grantor with its governing documents, a completed and filed IRS Form SS-4 or other documentation satisfactory to Grantor, showing Grantee's separate existence as an organization.

2. Grantee shall use the grant solely for the project described in the accompanying cover letter, and Grantee shall repay to Grantor any portion of the amount granted which is not used for that project. Any changes in the purposes for which grant funds are spent must be approved in writing by Grantor before implementation. Grantor retains the right, if Grantee breaches this Agreement, or if Grantee's conduct of the project jeopardizes Grantor's legal or tax status, to withhold, withdraw, or demand immediate return of grant funds, and to spend such funds so as to accomplish the purposes of the project as nearly as possible within Grantor's sole judgment. Any tangible or intangible property, including copyrights, obtained or created by Grantee as part of this project shall remain the property of Grantee.

3. Grantee may solicit gifts, contributions and grants to Grantor, earmarked for Grantor's restricted fund for this project. Grantee's choice of funding sources to be approached and the text of Grantee's fund-raising materials are sub-

---

*For optional provisions used in some Model C agreements, and for exemplars of Model A agreements and other transaction documents, visit www.silklaw.com.

---

ject to Grantor's prior written approval. All grant agreements, pledges, or other commitments with funding sources to support this project via Grantor's restricted fund shall be executed by Grantor. The cost of any reports or other compliance measures required by such funding sources shall be borne by Grantee.

4. An administrative charge of _____ percent (___%) of all amounts paid to Grantee from the restricted fund shall be deducted by Grantor to defray Grantor's costs of administering the restricted fund and this grant.

5. Nothing in this Agreement shall constitute the naming of Grantee as an agent or legal representative of Grantor for any purpose whatsoever except as specifically and to the extent set forth herein. This Agreement shall not be deemed to create any relationship of agency, partnership, or joint venture between the parties hereto, and Grantee shall make no such representation to anyone.

6. Grantee shall submit a full and complete report to Grantor as of the end of Grantee's annual accounting period within which any portion of this grant is received or spent. The initial report shall be submitted by Grantee no later than _____, 20__, and subsequent reports, if any, shall be due on the anniversary date of the initial report. The report shall describe the charitable programs conducted by the Grantee with the aid of this grant and the expenditures made with grant funds, and shall report on the Grantee's compliance with the terms of this grant.

7. This grant is not to be used in any attempt to influence legislation within the meaning of Internal Revenue Code (IRC) Section 501(c)(3). No agreement, oral or written, to that effect has been made between Grantor and Grantee.

Or, if the Grantor has evaluated the IRS limits imposed on Grantor's lobbying expenditures and has determined that part or all of the grant may be used for lobbying:

7. This grant is not to be used in any attempt to influence legislation within the meaning of IRC Section 501(c)(3), except for expenditures described in IRC Section 4911 as follows: Up to $_____ for grass-roots lobbying, and up to $_____ for all lobbying.

8. Grantee shall not use any portion of the funds granted herein to participate or intervene in any political campaign on behalf of or in opposition to any candidate for public office, to induce or encourage violations of law or public policy, to cause any private inurement or improper private benefit to

occur, nor to take any other action inconsistent with IRC Section 501(c)(3).

9. Grantee shall notify Grantor immediately of any change in (a) Grantee's legal or tax status, and (b) Grantee's executive or key staff responsible for achieving the grant purposes.

10. Grantee hereby irrevocably and unconditionally agrees, to the fullest extent permitted by law, to defend, indemnify and hold harmless Grantor, its officers, directors, trustees, employees and agents, from and against any and all claims, liabilities, losses and expenses (including reasonable attorneys' fees) directly, indirectly, wholly or partially arising from or in connection with any act or omission of Grantee, its employees or agents, in applying for or accepting the grant, in expending or applying the funds furnished pursuant to the grant or in carrying out the program or project to be funded or financed by the grant, except to the extent that such claims, liabilities, losses or expenses arise from or in connection with any act or omission of Grantor, its officers, directors, trustees, employees or agents.

11. [Clause providing for mediation or binding arbitration as an alternative to litigation, in the event of a dispute arising under the Agreement]

12. This Agreement shall be governed by and construed in accordance with the laws of the State of _____ applicable to agreements made and to be performed entirely within such State.

13. This Agreement shall supersede any prior oral or written understandings or communications between the parties and constitutes the entire agreement of the parties with respect to the subject matter hereof. This Agreement may not be amended or modified, except in a writing signed by both parties hereto.

IN WITNESS WHEREOF, the parties have executed this Grant Agreement effective on the _____ day of _____, 20__.

_____, Grantor

By:_____   Dated:

_____, Grantee

By:_____   Dated:

DEDUCTIBILITY OF CONTRIBUTIONS IRS REVENUE RULING 66-79 (1966-1 C.B. 48)

The Internal Revenue Service has been asked to clarify Revenue Ruling 63-252, C.B. 1963-2, 101, with respect to the deductibility of contributions to a domestic charitable corporation that may solicit contributions for a specific project of a foreign charity in the manner presented below.

X Corporation is a domestic charitable organization formed under the nonprofit laws of the state of Y. It is exempt from federal income tax as being organized and operated exclusively for charitable, educational and scientific purposes described in Section 501(c)(3) of the Internal Revenue Code of 1954. Contributions to it are deductible because it is an organization described in Section 170(c)(2) of the code.

The corporation's charter provides, in part, that in furtherance of its educational, scientific and charitable purposes it shall have the power to receive and allocate contributions, within the discretion of the board of directors, to any organization organized and operated exclusively for charitable or educational purposes within the meaning of Section 501(c)(3) of the code.

In contrast to the broad generality of the purposes stated in its charter, the name X Corporation suggests a purpose to assist a named foreign organization. The individuals who organized X Corporation had become interested in furthering the work of the named foreign organization, a corporation organized and operated in a foreign country exclusively for charitable, scientific and educational purposes. The individuals concerned, who are United States citizens not acting on behalf of the foreign organization, did not wish X Corporation to function simply as a fund-raising medium for the foreign organization. Instead, they were interested in raising funds for specific projects, such as scientific research projects, to be carried out by the foreign organization, or individuals connected with the foreign organization, pursuant to grants previously reviewed and approved by the board of directors of X Corporation.

The bylaws of X Corporation provide, in part, that: (1) The making of grants and contributions and otherwise rendering financial assistance for the purposes expressed in the charter of the organization shall be within the exclusive power of the board of directors; (2) in furtherance of the organization's purposes, the board of directors shall have power to make grants to any organization organized and operated exclusively for charitable, scientific or educational purposes within the meaning of Section 501(c)(3) of the code; (3) the board of directors shall review all requests for funds from other organizations, shall require that such requests specify the use to which the funds will be put, and if the board of directors approves the request, shall authorize payment of such funds to the approved grantee; (4) the board of directors shall require that the grantees furnish a periodic accounting to show that the funds were expended for the purposes that were approved by the board of directors; and (5) the board of directors may, in its absolute discretion, refuse to make any grants or contributions or otherwise render financial assistance to or for any or all of the purposes for which funds are requested.

The bylaws also provide that after the board of directors has approved a grant to another organization for a specific project or purpose, the corporation may solicit funds for the grant to the specifically approved project or purpose of the other organization. However, the board of directors shall at times have the right to withdraw approval of the grant and use the funds for other charitable, scientific or educational purpose.

In accordance with the provisions of its charter and bylaws, X Corporation at times solicits contributions that are to be used to provide grants to the foreign organization mentioned above, or to individuals connected with such foreign organization, for specific purposes approved by X Corporation's board of directors in accordance with its bylaws. At all times all of the pertinent facts, including the fact that the board of directors may withdraw its approval of a particular grant even after it has been made, are available to any contributor not previously informed of such facts should the contributor so request either before or after a contribution has been made. The corporation refuses to accept contributions so earmarked that they must in any event go to the foreign organization.

Section 170(a) of the code provides, in part, that there shall be allowed as a deduction any charitable contribution as defined in subsection (c), payment of which is made within the taxable year.

Section 170(c) of the code defines a charitable contribution as meaning, in part, a contribution or gift to or for the use of a corporation, trust, or community chest, fund or foundation which is organized and operated exclusively for religious, charitable, scientific, literary, or educational purposes or for the prevention of cruelty to children or animals. However, the organization must be created or organized in the United States, or in any possession thereof, or under the law of the United States, any State or Territory, the District of Columbia, or any possession of the United States.

Revenue Ruling 63-252, C.B. 1963-2, 101, discusses the deductibility of contributions by individuals to a charity organized in the United States which thereafter transmits some or all of its funds to a foreign charitable organization. Example (4) of that ruling concerns a domestic organization described in Section 170(c) of the code, which makes grants to a foreign organization for purposes that the domestic organization has reviewed and approved as in furtherance of its purposes. Contributions to the domestic organization are not earmarked in any manner for a foreign organization and the use of such contributions is subject to control by the domestic organization. For these reasons, the domestic organization is considered to be the recipient of such contributions within the meaning of Section 170(c)(2) of the code.

Under the provisions of its charter and bylaws, X Corporation may make grants to any organization organized and operated exclusively for charitable, scientific, or educational purposes within the meaning of Section 501(c)(3) of the code. An organization described in that section can be either a domestic or a foreign organization. The operations of X Corporation bring it within the purview of example (4) of Revenue Ruling 63-252 except for the manner in which it may solicit contributions for its foreign grants. This raises a question as to whether the contributions are earmarked for the foreign organization so as to prohibit a deduction under Section 170 of the code.

Revenue Ruling 62-113, C.B. 1962-2, 10, holds that where gifts to an organization described in Section 170(c) of the code are not earmarked by the donor for a particular individual, the deduction will be allowable where it is established that a gift is intended by the donor for the use of the organization and not as a gift to an individual for whose benefit the amount given may be used by the donee organization. The test in each case is whether the organization has full control of the donated funds, and discretion as to their use, so as to ensure that they will be used to carry out its functions and purposes.

In the instant case the domestic corporation may only solicit for specific grants when it has reviewed and approved them as being in furtherance of its purposes. Furthermore, under the terms of its bylaws, the domestic corporation may make such solicitations only on the condition that it shall have control and discretion as to the use of the contributions received by it. Therefore, contributions received by the domestic organization from such solicitations are regarded as for the use of the domestic corporation and not for the organization receiving the grant from the domestic organization.

Accordingly, contributions paid to the domestic organization under the circumstances described above are deductible, for federal income tax purposes, in the manner and to the extent provided by Section 170 of the code.

Revenue Ruling 63-252 is hereby amplified.

COMMENTARY
ON TAXABILITY OF GRANTS

Acomprehensive analysis of the taxability of various forms of grants is beyond the scope of this book, even though the issue is often critical to the choice of fiscal sponsorship method. The following discussion is intended to highlight some of the issues involved.

Section 61 of the Internal Revenue Code defines "gross income" as "income from whatever source derived," except as specifically excluded by other provisions in the code. Section 63 defines "taxable income" as gross income minus permitted deductions. Thus, unless some or all of the grant falls within one of the exceptions, a grant must be included in full in the recipient's taxable income. Whether any of the statutory exceptions apply to any particular grant (or portions thereof) depends on the purposes of the grant, the types of expenses covered, the structure of the relationship between the grantor and the grantee, and the nature of the grantor and the grantee. Some of the statutory exceptions that may apply to grants received by individuals are:

• Section 74(b) excludes from gross income prizes and awards made primarily in recognition of religious, charitable, scientific, educational, artistic, literary or civic achievement, if (1) the recipient took no action to enter the contest or proceeding resulting in the award, (2) the award is not conditioned on future services being rendered by the recipient, and (3) the recipient designates a governmental unit or charity to receive the award. Otherwise, prizes and awards are included in taxable income.

• Section 117 excludes from taxable income certain scholarship and fellowship grants received by degree candidates attending qualified educational institutions. To be tax-free, the grant must be used for tuition and related expenses, as defined by the Code and regulations thereunder.

• Section 139 excludes from gross income payments made to pay or reimburse unreimbursed reasonable and necessary medical, temporary housing, or transportation expenses relating to certain disasters. See also Revenue Ruling 2003-12.

- Section 102 generally excludes gifts (as defined in the Code) from taxable income. While this exception usually will not apply to grants, it may apply to some hardship relief payments not otherwise excluded under the Code.

- Section 104 generally excludes certain payments received as compensation for personal injuries or sickness. This exception usually will not apply to grants.

In addition to the foregoing statutory exclusions, some grants do not fall within the definition of income because the grant represents reimbursement or advancement for expenses. For example, in Revenue Ruling 59-92, the IRS reviewed a grant made by a tax-exempt county heart association to an individual as principal investigator and administrator of a research program. The researcher spent the grant as required by its terms to cover costs of the research; the researcher received no salary or other economic benefit from the grant. The IRS found that none of the grant should be included in the individual's gross income. The same logic is evident in Revenue Ruling 77-279, Situation 1. There, the IRS considered a situation in which an individual rendered gratuitous day care services for needy children, and the charity reimbursed or advanced expenses to the individual incurred in connection with providing the services. The IRS stated that the services were being incurred "on behalf and for the use of" the charity, and need not be included in gross income of the recipient, provided specified conditions are met.

Finally, independent of the Code, certain kinds of payments are exempt from federal income taxation under the U.S. Constitution or a currently effective act of Congress. For example, this includes payments made by a city or state to the needy, or for child care, or awards to crime victims. It is possible that one of these provisions might apply to exclude a particular grant from the grantee's taxable income.

Because of the variety and specificity of legal provisions that may affect the taxability of a grant to the grantee, both within the Code and elsewhere, if the issue is important, the grantee should consult an attorney or accountant with expertise in the nonprofit area to review its individual tax situation.

| Robert Wexler | Silk, Adler & Colvin |
| Shirley Chin | March 2005 |

QUALIFICATIONS FOR PUBLIC CHARITY STATUS
IRC §509(a)(3) SUPPORTING ORGANIZATION

Tax-exempt status under Section 501(c)(3) of the Internal Revenue Code permits a charitable organization to pay no tax on any operating surplus it may have at the end of a year, and it permits donors to claim a charitable deduction for their contributions.

A further division among 501(c)(3) organizations classifies them into private foundations and public charities. Private foundations come under Chapter 42 of the IRC, which imposes a nominal tax on net investment income, limits self-dealing and business holdings, requires minimum annual distributions, prohibits lobbying entirely, and restricts the organization's operations in other ways. Also, large donors to a private foundation have a less favorable ceiling on the amount of deductible gifts they can claim each year.

Clearly, it is better to be a public charity, although some 501(c)(3)s prefer private foundation status to maintain their dominant funding relationship with one person, family or corporation, and their independence, in spite of the restrictions.

A 501(c)(3) organization can avoid private foundation status, and thus be classified as a public charity, 1) by being a certain kind of institution, such as a church, school or hospital, or 2) by meeting one of two mathematical public support tests. If a 501(c)(3) cannot meet those qualifications, it can still be a public charity if it is a supporting organization to another 501(c)(3) that does.[21] This status is defined by Section 509(a)(3) of the Internal Revenue Code.

---

[21] This status is also available to a 501(c)(3) that supports a (c)(4) social welfare organization, a (c)(5) labor union, or a (c)(6) trade association, that has enough diversified sources of funds to meet the second of the two mathematical tests. Some tests differ slightly for non-(c)(3) support relationships.

This outline is designed to help your organization consider whether it could qualify to be a public charity under Section 509(a)(3), as a supporting organization to one or more other organizations. There are four tests to satisfy. In the outline, X = the supporting organization, Y = one or more supported organizations.

I. **The Relationship Test.** One of the following three relationship tests must be met:

   A. X is operated, supervised or controlled by Y. A parent-subsidiary relationship. Typically, a majority of the board of directors of X is appointed by Y. (Type 1)

   B. X is supervised or controlled in connection with Y. This is a brother-sister relationship. Control or management of X and Y must be vested in the same persons. (Type 2)

   C. X is operated in connection with Y. The required degree of control is more attenuated. (Type 3) Both of two subtests must be met:

      1. *The responsiveness test.* X must be responsive to the needs or demands of Y, to be shown in one of two ways:

      a. Y selects at least one director of X, or X and Y have a director in common, or there is a close and continuing relationship between the leaders of X and Y; plus Y thereby has a significant voice in X's investment policies, grantmaking and other uses of X's income or assets. OR

      b. X is a charitable trust under state law, Y is a beneficiary with power to enforce the trust and compel an accounting by X.

      AND

      2. *The integral part test.* X must be significantly involved in the affairs of Y, so that Y is dependent on X, to be shown in one of two ways:

      a. X directly engages in activities that perform the functions of or carry out the purposes of Y, and would normally be conducted by Y; e.g., a publishing house for a university. OR

      b. X pays at least 85% of its income to or for the use of Y, and this amount is important enough to Y to ensure that Y will be attentive to the operations of X.

II. **The Organizational Test.** The governing instrument of X (e.g. articles of incorporation) must comply with all four of these requirements:

A. *Purposes.* X must be organized exclusively for the benefit of, to perform the functions of, or to carry out the purposes of one or more qualified public charities.

B. *Activities.* X must not be empowered to engage in activities other than those stated above.

C. *Specification of the Supported Organization.* Y must be named as the organization on whose behalf X will be operated, but if the relationship is parent-subsidiary or brother-sister, then the supported organization[s] can be designated by class or purpose rather than by name.

D. *Other Organizations.* X must not be empowered to support or benefit any organization other than those specified above.

III. **The Operational Test.** X may make payments to or for the use of Y, make grants, conduct independent programs, raise funds, and engage in unrelated trade or business. However, permissible beneficiaries of its grants or programs are limited to:

A. Y itself, which may be multiple supported organizations specified by name or class.

B. Individual members of the charitable class served by Y. The payment or benefit may be given directly, or earmarked for the person and given through an unrelated organization.

C. Other Section 509(a)(3) organizations that support Y.

D. Public colleges and universities.

IV. **The Control Test.** X may not be controlled, directly or indirectly, by those persons or entities listed below. Control means either 50% of the combined voting power on the board of X, or veto power over the activities of X, unless it can be shown that actual control rests elsewhere; e.g., with the bishop of a church. Those who are prohibited from control are:

A. A substantial contributor (any person or entity who gives more than the greater of $5,000 or 2% of the total gifts received by X including gifts from a spouse).

B. If X is a trust, the creator of the trust.

C. An owner of more than 20% of a corporation, partnership, trust or other enterprise that is a substantial contributor to X.

D. A member of the family of any person described in A, B or C (spouses, ancestors, children, grandchildren and great-grandchildren, and all of their spouses).

E. A corporation, partnership or trust in which persons described in A, B, C or D hold more than 35% of the voting power, profits interest, or beneficial interest, respectively.

F. Employees of any of the above.

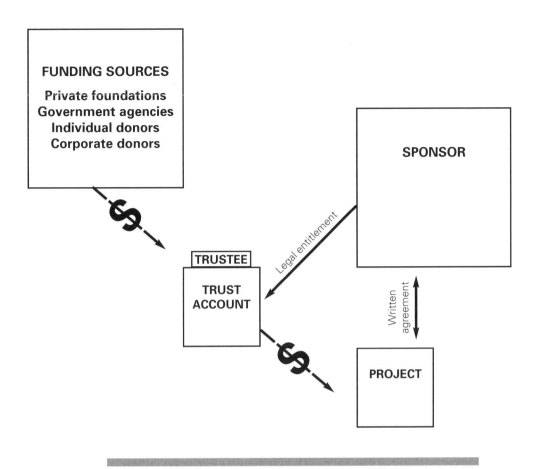

FUNDING SOURCES

Private foundations
Government agencies
Individual donors
Corporate donors

SPONSOR

TRUSTEE

TRUST
ACCOUNT

Legal entitlement

Written
agreement

PROJECT

MODEL X — PAYMENTS "FOR THE USE OF" SPONSOR

This model has not been used much outside of the Mormon church, but it offers the possibility of a form of fiscal sponsorship with a much lower level of accounting and tax reporting, at least for the sponsor. In fact, the Mormon church itself has moved away from the trust concept and toward a collective pool arrangement that supports missionaries in both high and low living expense areas. Model X should be undertaken only with specialized legal advice, and perhaps a private letter ruling should be sought from the IRS before proceeding.

Among the hypothetical cases, the best candidate for Model X is the Mormon missionary working with the FBRF in the Brazilian jungle, whose parents could establish a trust "for the use" of the Mormon church to support her work among native people.

Model X is suggested in a 1990 U.S. Supreme Court opinion written by Justice Sandra Day O'Connor for a unanimous court in *Davis v. United States.*[22] In this case, the IRS challenged the method by which most Mormon missionaries receive financial aid from their parents. The young missionaries, who receive no salary from the Mormon church, typically pay their own living and travel expenses out of their own savings or out of funds sent directly to them by their parents. The parents claim the payments as tax-deductible charitable contributions, even though the money does not pass through the church, relying on language in Internal Revenue Code Section 170, which permits deductions for donations to or for the use of religious and other charitable organizations.

The Supreme Court ruled in favor of the IRS, but it did not require that donations, to be deductible, only be made to the immediate possession and control of the Mormon church. It interpreted the phrase "for the use of" to refer to donations made to a legally enforceable trust or similar legal arrangement, separate from the charity but established for the benefit of the charity. The court found that the typical Mormon missionary arrangement fell short, because:

• The parents transfer the money to their sons' personal bank accounts on which the sons are the sole signatories.

• The parents took no steps normally associated with creating a trust or similar legal arrangement.

• Although the sons promise to use the money in accordance with church guidelines, they do not have any legal obligation to do so. There was no evidence that the guidelines had any legally binding effect.

• The church does not appear to have a legal entitlement to the money

---

[22] 495 U.S. 472, 110 S.Ct. 2014, 109 L.Ed.2d 457, 90-1 USTC ¶50270 (1990).

or a civil cause of action against missionaries who use their parents' money for purposes not approved by the church.

Justice O'Connor's opinion, then, seems to prescribe four requirements for an intriguing fiscal sponsorship method where the funds to support a project do not have to pass through the sponsoring charity:

1. Take the steps normally associated with creating a trust or similar legal arrangement (e.g., execute a written trust document), for the benefit of the sponsor.

2. To handle donations, set up a bank account for the trust or similar arrangement, upon which the individuals conducting the project are not the sole signatories.

3. Have the individuals involved with the project sign a legally binding agreement with the sponsor, obligating them to use the funds in the trust or similar arrangement according to the sponsor's guidelines.

4. In the written document creating the trust or similar arrangement, provide for the sponsor to be legally entitled to take possession of the money (at any time, or upon certain conditions); OR give the sponsor a civil cause of action against the individuals conducting the project if they use the money for purposes not approved by the sponsor.

> ## What will IRS require?
>
> It is not known what additional requirements, beyond these four, may be required by the IRS for missionary trusts. In Technical Advice Memorandum 9149005, the IRS rejected two Mormon missionary trusts, partly because the class of potential beneficiaries was too small (descendants of certain persons). The church was not named as the beneficiary.

Relationship

In the situation of the Mormon church, the work of the mission is part of the direct program of the church, carried out by unpaid volunteer missionaries. The church supervises many aspects of their daily, personal lives. So, if we are to design a fiscal sponsorship model by precise analogy to the Mormon missionary fact pattern, the model is more likely to withstand IRS scrutiny if the project is a closely controlled program of the sponsor.

However, the *Davis* decision seems to indicate that a trust or similar arrangement works even if the project is an indirect program of the sponsor, such as a grantee project, so long as there is a legally binding agreement to follow the sponsor's program guidelines. If the project is not an integral part of the sponsor's program, it could establish something like the preapproved grant relationship by following the seven-step process, leading to a trust agreement signed by the project, and by the sponsor as legal beneficiary of the trust supporting the project.

Handling of Charitable Donations

It may take some convincing to persuade private foundations,[23] government agencies, corporate and individual donors that a payment not made "to" the sponsor but to a separate trust account "for the use of" the sponsor is just as proper and deductible. The sponsor should review fund-raising solicitations, and it may be bound by the project's representations. But, ordinarily, the funds raised will not actually be the property of the sponsor. The funds will go directly to the trust or similar arrangement and will be spent out of that account for the project's expenses, subject only to the potentiality that the sponsor may decide to take over the funds at some point. Undoubtedly, the attorney general would consider such a separate fund to be subject to the state law of charitable trusts.

Administrative Charge

A sponsor could levy an administrative charge for the approval, monitoring and other overhead processes involved with sponsoring the project. However, the charge may be harder to collect, because in this scenario the sponsor does not actually have possession of the funds, even temporarily, unless something goes wrong.

Liabilities

The Mormon missionaries are legally agents of, and by their acts or omissions they can create liabilities for, the Mormon church. The extent of the sponsor's liabilities depends on whether the project is an integral part of the sponsor's direct program or whether the sponsor has succeeded in establishing a more distant, indirect relationship with only those controls needed to satisfy

---

[23] A grant by a private foundation must be "to" a public charity under Internal Revenue Code §4945(d)(4), but if expenditure responsibility is exercised, the grant can be made to a separate entity or project "for the use of" a public charity or for any charitable purpose.

federal tax law. But if the legal contract gives the sponsor certain supervisory rights in order to ensure that project funds are spent to serve its purposes, and the sponsor negligently fails to enforce those rights, causing harm to another, the sponsor conceivably could be held liable.

Ownership

Like the issue of liability, the question of ownership will depend on what is stated in the agreement between the sponsor and the project. What should be stated, consistent with the *Davis* decision, is that the sponsor retains the right to come in and take possession of any assets acquired or created by the project.

Tax Reporting

Unlike Models A, B and C, Model X does not call for the sponsor to show the project trust or similar arrangement among its assets on IRS Form 990, unless the sponsor has taken the step of assuming possession of the project's assets. Nor would the revenues and expenditures of the project trust ordinarily appear on the sponsor's Form 990. The relief from this accounting burden was one of the main reasons the Mormon church preferred that parents support their missionary children, who number more than 40,000 each year, through a system of direct payments.

For the project itself, it is not yet clear what, if any, reporting obligation it may have. The tax accounting for *Davis*-type project trusts will have to be settled as experiments with this arrangement are developed.

APPLYING MODEL X TO THE HYPOTHETICALS

#1 — The Artists

The main difficulty with applying Model X to Amparo's and Keith's projects is the fact that the consortium is not likely to exercise nearly the degree of control over a dance troupe or an independent film project that the Mormon church exercises over its missionaries. Therefore, contributions to a trust account established to fund an art project might not be seen as "for the use of" the consortium.

Nevertheless, if the *Davis* case is broadly interpreted to allow more distant control arrangements, project trusts may be a viable alternative to the grant relationship. The main benefit would be that the funds for the project would not have to flow through the consortium's accounting system. If the consortium is sponsoring 100 separate arts projects, reducing its accounting burden would be a great relief. However, the consortium might have an increased monitoring burden, to make sure trust funds are properly handled and to place them in receivership if they are not.

For Amparo and Keith, Model X may restrict them more than the grant relationship. They will not have independent signature power over the trust account, and they will always be subject to the possibility that the sponsor may take possession of the trust account funds or even the entire project.

#2 — The Human Services Project

Model X is probably not a good fit for the hospice and the church. The hospice project is larger and will last longer than would be suitable for a project trust account. The hospice needs its own corporate entity, either for-profit or nonprofit, to carry out its work.

#3 — The Environmental Group

Obviously, Model X is best suited for the support of the Mormon missionary working in the Brazilian jungle. Under the *Davis* ruling, her parents will have to work with the church to establish a trust account, rather than sending money directly to her, if they want a charitable tax deduction.

Model X also might work for Holly's donation and the short-term project she wants to support. If the foundation established guidelines for the project and a trust agreement with the necessary enforcement provisions, a trust account to which Holly would directly contribute could be set up. Funds from the trust account would be disbursed in Brazil, with expenditure reports sent back to the foundation for accountability. If administered properly, Holly's charitable contribution to a trust "for the use of" the foundation would be valid without ever having to be recorded on the financial statement or tax return of the foundation or FBRF.

INDEX

Hume, Leslie, viii
Hutton, William, 77n.18

Incubation, 64, 70–71
  fund-raising for, 80
  in preapproved grant relationship, 77
Incubators, 14
Independent contractor project model (Model
      B), 10, 21–22, 21–26
  administrative charge in, 23
  application to hypotheticals of, 24–26
  characteristics and relationship of, 12–13
  handling charitable donations in, 23
  liabilities of, 23
  ownership in, 23
  popularity of, 67–69
  relationship of, 22
  tax reporting in, 24
Independent contractors, work made for hire, 78
Injury payments, taxability of, 92
Insurance, for direct project, 69, 73–74
Intangible assets, of direct project, 19, 77
Integral part test, 94
Intellectual property, 23, 77–78
Intermediary, 64, 76
Internal Revenue Code (IRC)
  501(c)(3) status, v, 2–4
  501(c)(4) status, 8, 75
  Section 61, 91–92
  Section 63, 91
  Section 74(b), 91
  Section 102, 92
  Section 104, 92
  Section 117, 91
  Section 139, 91–92
  Section 170, 89–90
  Section 170(a), 89
  Section 170(c), 89
  Section 509(a)(3), 50-52, 93-96
  Section 7701(1), 65n.5
Internal Revenue Service (IRS)
  anti-conduit policies of, 3, 65–67
  501(c)(3) classification, 93–96
  free-standing, 49–50
  as public charity, 52n.32
  501(c)(3) tax status, obtaining, 42–43
  charity classifications of, 3–4, 46–47
  conduit organizations under, 3, 65–67

fiscal agent treatment by, 64–67
Form 990, 16, 35n.17, 46–47
  for grant payments, 35–36
  Schedule A, Part IV, 52
Form 1040, 16
  Schedules C and SE, 36
  for sole proprietorship, 24
Form 1099, for grant payments, 35–36
Form 1099-MISC, 35n.18
Form SS-4, 31
Publication 1779, 22
recognition of fiscal sponsorship, 81–82
Rev. Proc., 80-27, 1980-1 C.B. 677, 43n.27
Rev. Rul., 66-103, 34
Rev. Rul., 63-252, 89–90
Rev. Rul., 66-79, 76
  deductibility of contributions, 87–90
Rev. Rul., 77-279, 92
tax exemption of sponsorship relationships,
    61
for technical assistance, 54–55
International fiscal sponsorship, 75n.16
Intersection for the Arts, viii, x, xi

Johnson, George, 81
Joint funding collaboratives, 71–72
Joint venture, 64
Jones, David, 81

Kreidler, John, vii, viii, xii

Laundering donations, 64, 65–66
Layton, Tom, vii, xii
Leaving the nest, 18–20, 74–75
Lehrfeld, Bill, vii, ix
Levy, Mort, vii
Liabilities
  in direct project model, 16, 69
  in fiscal sponsorship models, 13
  in group exemption model, 45–46
  identifying, 19
  in independent contract project model, 23
  method of transferring, 20
  in payments "for the use of" sponsor model,
      100–101
  in preapproved grant relationship model,
      33–34
  in supporting organization model, 52

in technical assistance model, 57
Link, Geoff, vii, viii
Lobbying
    IRS allowance for, 78
    of tax-exempt entity, 39

Mackaman, Julie, vii, viii
Management contract, 12
Management services, 68n.11
Masaoka, Jan, viii
Media Network, 73
Model A. *See* Direct project model
Model B. *See* Independent project model
Model C. *See* Preapproved grant relationship model
Model D. *See* Group exemption model
Model E. *See* Supporting organization model
Model F. *See* Technical assistance model
Model X. *See* Payments "for the use of" sponsor model
Mormon church missionaries
    in *Davis* case, 98–102
    liability of, 100–101
    ruling on, 11
    sponsor relationship in, 99–100
    trust for missionary work, 68,69, 102

National Endowment for the Arts, 63
New York Foundation for the Arts, xi
National Foundation case, 33n.15
Nonprofits
    dynamism of, 61
    group exemption of, 42–43
    objectives of, xi
    projects sponsored by, xi

O'Connor, Sandra Day, 98
O'Neill, Michael, vii
Operational test, 50, 95
Organizational test, 50, 94–95
Ottawa Silicia v. U.S., 40n.25
Owens, Marc, vii, ix
Owl Foundation case, 65–66

Partnership, 64
    of artists, 36–37
    tax returns for, 24
Pass-through, 64

Payments "for the use of" sponsor model
    (Model X), 11, 68–69, 97–99
    administrative charge in, 100
    application to hypotheticals of, 101–102
    characteristics and relationship of, 12–13
    handling of charitable donations in, 100
    liabilities in, 100–101
    ownership in, 101
    relationship in, 99–100
    tax reporting in, 101
Payroll taxes, 15, 16
Phillips, Frances, vii, viii
Pike, Drummond, vii, ix, 60
Platforms, 64, 72
Pledges, 79–80
Preapproved grant relationship model (Model
    C), 10, 27–41, 75–77
    accounting, discretion and control in, 75–77
    administrative charge in, 33
    application to hypotheticals of, 36–41
    array of projects in, 75
    characteristics and relationship of, 12–13
    criticism of, 60
    handling of charitable donations in, 31–33
    incubation in, 77
    liabilities in, 33–34
    misunderstandings in, 27–28
    ownership in, 35
    popularity of, 67–69
    relationship in, 29–31
    tax reporting in, 35–36
Private benefit prohibition, 61
Prizes, taxability of, 91
Progress and Freedom Foundation, 72
Project grant reports, 30
Public agency, 64
Public charity status, 44, 49–50
    qualifications for, 93–96
    section 509(a)(3), 52

Regranting, 27–28, 64
Relationship test, 50, 94
Responsiveness test, 94
Restricted fund, 32–33
Risk management, for direct project, 69
Roady, Celia, ix
Robinson, Alma, vii